Praise for Kate Christie

'We brought together an incredible line-up of international business owners and speakers to inspire our audience of 400+ British female entrepreneurs to back themselves and keep creating amazing businesses. Kate Christie from Time Stylers absolutely met our brief. She is an expert in time investment and an incredibly dynamic speaker. The feedback from all of our audiences was overwhelmingly positive. Kate is an absolute professional.'

Ciara Fitzgerald, Innovation and Business Adviser Team Manager, Enterprise Europe Network, Newable

'Some speakers are all hype and little substance. Not Kate Christie—her content was 'gold'. She showed the audience how to create an extra 30 hours of productive time every month without having to work more hours. Think about that: 30 hours is an extra two or three days that can be used for family time, or for producing results and more income. If time is money, an extra 30 hours per month, 360 hours per year, is worth a fortune to a focused professional. You can understand why our audience took notes furiously!'

Gary Pittard, CEO, Pittard

'Kate Christie a time saving dynamo—a super hero of time management and getting organised.'

Kochie's Business Builders

'We needed a dynamic and engaging speaker to present to our Women in Business customers. A colleague recommended Kate to us and she was both insightful and inspirational. With her vibrant and fun personality, Kate connected with our audience immediately and delivered content that they could use when they get back to their office. Kate was very easy to work with. She delivered clear, strong and practical messages with humour and certainly retained the attention of our guests.'

Erika Perkins,
Regional General Manager,
Westpac Retail Banking Victoria

Praise for **Me Time**

'As a mom with a portfolio career, I always burn the candle at both ends. This book made me pause and then hit the Me First button for self care.'

Anoushka

'Any working mom knows how hard it is to find 'Me Time'. In this book you'll find practical strategies to help you recover time for you. Great read and practical tips you can implement immediately.'

Caroline

'This is a great guide, especially for working moms. Personally I find it really hard to find "Me time" as I need to take care of my own business and my child. However, this book gives great time-management tips. Kate knows what she is talking about. This book is a must read!'

Cynthia

'We all want more time - finally a book that delivers!'

Katrina

'I am a huge fan of Kate Christie's work - she is open, honest, funny, and 100 per cent practical - nothing is sugar coated. And when you are a busy mom, wife, professional (and the other 100 hats we wear), you need to hear it straight.'

Emma

'Work & life are such a juggle and to gain time back to do what's really important is gold. A great read!'

Jane

'Finally, a book that gives me permission to add Me! to the list of important people that I happily give my precious time and support to.'

Sam

First published in 2020 by John Wiley & Sons Australia, Ltd
42 McDougall St, Milton Qld 4064

Office also in Melbourne

Typeset in 11pt/14pt Adobe Caslon Pro Regular

ISBN: 978-0-730-38400-7

A catalogue record for this book is available from the National Library of Australia

Cover design by Wiley

Printed in the USA by Sheridan, KY, A, CJK Group Company

SKYC70DE261-A4AD-4D98-8CF3-C4F6B2CD6C65_072020

Disclaimer

ME FIRST

The Guilt-free Guide to Prioritising You

KATE CHRISTIE

WILEY

To time-poor women everywhere, it's time to start thinking about your time the way you think about your money: as a precious, enormously valuable and limited resource that needs to be consciously invested for the greatest possible return.

And in memory of Jane Christina Ferris, my beautiful mom and greatest fan. I miss you.

Contents

Why it's time for Me First *xi*

Part I: The mistakes we make – what could get in the way? 1

Our afflictions: Where we waste our time 3
Mistake #1: Imposter syndrome 9
Mistake #2: Busy lifestyle syndrome 14
Mistake #3: Superwoman syndrome 17
Mistake #4: *Yes* syndrome 21
Mistake #5: Judgement 26
Mistake #6: Guilt 32
Mistake #7: It's easier if I just do it myself 36
Mistake #8: My kids aren't going to make this easy 37
Mistake #9: My partner is the problem! 39
Mistake #10: I was told I could have it all. What happened? 40
Mistake #11: I don't need help 42
Mistake #12: I just don't know where to start 44
Mistake #13: I don't have time for me 45

Part II: The 5 SMART Steps 49

All about Alice 51
The 5 SMART Steps: an overview 55

Step 1: Self-aware 61
Step 2: Map 89
Step 3: Analyse 103
Step 4: Reframe 121
Step 5: Take control 153

Part III: How about a little bonus? 159

How to set and smash audacious goals 161
Where to now? 171

About Kate *173*
Work with Kate *175*
Acknowledgements *179*
Index *181*

Why it's time for *Me First*

I published my first book—*Me Time: The professional woman's guide to finding 30 guilt-free hours a month*—in 2014. It became a best-selling book and literally changed my life. However, a lot of additional life-changing and not-so-life-changing events have occurred in my life since 2014, all of which prompted me to update, enhance and push the concept of Me Time further—to embrace a state of 'Me First':

- My marriage ended after 22 years, and I suddenly found myself a single mom to three teenagers. Everything I had planned for—my future, our collective future—was suddenly, and quite simply, gone. I personally needed to reframe.
- The Universe, which I must say I had never previously held much store in, was watching closely and decided to give my business a bit of a nudge—thank you, Universe.
- My beautiful mom passed away and left a huge hole in our family.
- Having shared my framework—The 5 SMART Steps—with tens of thousands of people around the world, I have

collected so many stories from amazing women, and so many incredible insights that I want to share with you. One of the best things about being an author of a self-help book, and working in an industry where your number-one goal is to educate and motivate people on how to change their lives for the better, is the number of people who willingly share their personal stories with you. It is validating for me, but more importantly, it provides me with so many extra data points I can share with you to help you on your own personal journey to taking control of your time.

- There is more time to be had. In *Me Time* I promised and delivered 30 hours of lost time a month. In *Me First*, if you are up for it, there is even more time up for grabs.
- After getting their lost time back, many of my clients want my help in framing the right goals for where they are going to invest their new-found time—so I am going to share my goal-setting framework with you, too.

The rules

Me Time was a good start. It helped you reflect on your poor time habits, take control of your time by implementing better time habits and to find 30 hours of lost time a month. But it's not enough. Because while you may have taken those tentative steps towards prioritising yourself some of the time, you continue to do so with a lot of guilt. Moreover, there is not much point in reclaiming hours of lost time if you are going to waste that time worrying that you are an imposter, that you should be doing better, or judging your self-worth based on someone else's opinion of you and your choices. Nor is it of value to find 30 hours of lost time if you are just going to fill those reclaimed hours doing more and more for others while neglecting yourself.

'Me Time' actually means 'Me First'. It's time to put yourself first. It's time to genuinely prioritise you. And this takes courage. It particularly takes courage as a mom because from the minute that little baby is born you are programmed to put your baby's needs before your own. For many, and maybe for you, becoming a mom means forever after coming second. Sleep? Forget it, that little baby needs you now. Food? Forget it, that little baby needs you now. Space? Forget it, that little baby needs you now. We become so used to putting our children's basic needs before our own basic needs, that it becomes second nature to then put all of their needs before any of our own. We give, and give, and then we give some more.

At some point in time—let's say, today—you need to be courageous. You need to find the courage to put yourself first, instead of second, third or fourth. You need to find the courage to carve out—to demand—time for yourself.

So, here are the rules:

- *It's time to take control of your time.* It's time to stop letting life just happen to you. It's time to make time for yourself. It's time to start putting yourself first. Because one thing I know for sure: if you don't demand this for yourself, no-one is going to do it for you.

- *Take action*. At every stage of reading *Me First*, reflect on what you agree with, what you don't agree with but makes you think hard about what's most important to you, and what you are going to do differently.

- *Family is a team sport.* From this moment on, your family needs to step up. I am more than happy to take one for the team (Team Mom) on this one—so feel free to blame me.

From today, Me Time means Me First. Get used to it.

How is *Me First* different?

Thanks to the thousands of you who have shared your stories with me since I first published *Me Time* because this gives me a lot more to share with my readers. For everyone else, please email me at info@timestylers.com and share how you have taken control of your time!

Over the past few years I have also surveyed (anonymously) every single audience for each of my speaking engagements around the world, both prior to the event (to find out what their key time pain points are, how many hours they work, what sorts of tasks they don't perform for lack of time and so on) and after the event (to ascertain what they have changed about how they invest their time as a result of what they now know about my unique framework—The 5 SMART Steps—a proven five-step process to help you find and harness hours of lost time). I have also reviewed thousands of individual time maps (see step 2 of The 5 SMART Steps). All of these data points have helped inform *Me First*.

One issue which is really apparent, and disturbing, from your stories is just how much pressure we continue to put on ourselves to be perfect. How much we juggle. How often we turn up. How busy we are. How often the buck stops with us. How stressed, anxious and exhausted we are. And just how many of us compound this by feeling that we are not doing any of it particularly well. Really? To double down on this, it is also alarming how often we feel judged for the choices we make as professional women with children. And don't get me started (just yet) on the guilt. This has to stop.

Part I of *Me First* explores these issues in far more depth than *Me Time* and offers stories and opinions from women across the globe—some high profile, many not. I want to share as many of their stories as possible, in part to help you realise that you are not alone—so that collectively we can laugh and cry at the crazy things we often do—and so that we know that it's okay to let our guard down and talk openly to each other about topics such as superwoman syndrome, mothers' guilt, being judged and imposter syndrome. Until we start talking about these topics and openly challenging them, nothing is going to change. Let's leave a better legacy for our daughters.

Part II of *Me First* takes you through The 5 SMART Steps with the goal of ridding yourself of time-wasting tasks and ensuring you reclaim 30 plus hours of lost time a month. There are exercises for each step that will challenge you to reveal your underlying drivers and desires in life. It is critical that you complete each and every exercise because this is where your brain takes the printed words in *Me First* and transfers them into your real-time world. Only you can do this. Your home life, your work life, your family life, your personal interests and the language you use are all unique to you. Besides, the exercises are where the gold is buried.

Part III of *Me First* contains a bonus: goal setting!

I want you to read *Me First*, absorb the underlying messages, undertake the exercises and take action to reclaim 30 plus hours of lost time a month. I want you to start living the life you want. Getting your lost time back will take work—but if you don't dig a little, then you won't find the nuggets.

In return, here are my five promises to you:

1. The 5 SMART Steps is a proven framework that has worked for tens of thousands of people. If you are ready to take action, The 5 SMART Steps will work for you too.

2. *Me First* provides simple, smart and sustainable solutions to find lost time, identify your poor time habits and implement better time habits.

3. *Me First* is targeted at clever, successful women who are also moms. You will work out what's most important to you and quantify the cost of what's not important. You will be left with absolute clarity over where you do, and do not, want to invest your time.

4. I will challenge you to stop wasting your time on the useless, self-destructive, low-value nonsense.
5. I don't do fluff and nonsense. I know you are (currently) time poor and that you want to hear it straight. Happily, that's my style. My goal is to leave you educated, entertained and with a lasting impact on the way you choose to live, work and play.

I know you

I know you. I know your time habits. I know your time challenges. I know your kids. I know your partner. I know what you do at work. I know what you don't do at work for lack of time. I can see you bouncing around all day like a shiny silver ball in a pinball machine. I know exactly what is getting in your way and I am going to tell you straight how to take control of your time. In some cases, especially when it comes to getting help from your kids and partner, some of my strategies are going to sound manipulative. I'm okay with that, because they are manipulative.

While you have all the appearance of absolute success in everything you do, scratch below the surface and the reality is that you are struggling, even just a little. Most time-poor, successful women who are also moms live with a constant undercurrent of stress and guilt. However, consistent with buying into the superwoman myth, you think you need to do it all. And so you don't change. Or, if you do try to change, you generally make unrealistic and unsustainable promises to yourself and, like embarking on a crash diet, you quickly fall back into old habits and feel worse for the failed attempt.

It's okay. You aren't alone.

We are all sick of the constant juggle. We have confused having it all with doing it all. We have forgotten that having it all really just means having all the bits that are most important to us. Throughout

Me First you will hear from women I interviewed for their insights on how they invest their time. I hope their advice and learnings resonate with you and that you draw inspiration from them.

So, when was the last time you just stopped and enjoyed the moment? Or did something for yourself that didn't involve work, favours for others or your family? Or looked forward to going out instead of falling into bed exhausted? Or didn't beat yourself up for your choices? You have lost sight of what's important to you. You have all these amazing balls in the air and yet you have no time to enjoy them because all of your focus is on the juggle.

Hell yes, you are damned clever and successful. But lady, that does not make you smart.

I was you

The reason I know you and why I know that I can help you, is that I was you and I fixed myself.

I am one of a generation of clever women who was told I could *have it all*. If you want it — they said — go and get it. My simple formula for success through school, university and into employment was hard work plus a massive amount of drive plus a modicum of talent, and I could pretty much have whatever I wanted. And it worked.

I was a superwoman. Then.

It all started to come unstuck between the years 2000 and 2003 when I had three babies in three-and-a-half years, all while trying to maintain my career and juggle work, a husband and a home. I don't expect any sympathy for this; I should have worked out what was happening at least after baby number two.

But hell, I didn't let that stop me. For five years straight my poor body was either pregnant or breastfeeding or both. I was frazzled, exhausted and working like a crazy woman trying to be the best of everything to everyone. Best career girl, best mom, best wife, best home maker … somewhere in there I forgot about being the best version of me.

Something had to give, and it did—big time. It was a Monday morning, and being a supermom as well as generally being a superwoman, I delayed my departure for work so that I could drop my son at school. Other moms do this all the time, right?

So, there I was, in my beautiful black suit, red lipstick, high heels and with snot from my shoulder to my knee with a hysterical child clinging to my leg because it was 'cupcake day'. (I don't know who comes up with these ideas—it certainly isn't moms who work.) Clearly, I did not have any cupcakes. I must have missed the memo.

Later, radiating guilt, covered in snot and thinking about the 25 years of cupcake therapy my son would need, I rushed (late) into my first meeting of the day. It took me a few seconds to register that the room was silent (maybe it was the snot). Everyone around the boardroom table looked at me and then looked at their watches, and then they resumed the meeting. And I had the profound realisation that I was the only member of the executive leadership team who didn't have a full-time wife.

Much of those years is a fog.

In trying to do it all I had lost sight of what was most important to me. I did not set appropriate boundaries and I never lived in the moment either at home or at work—if I was at work, I felt guilty about not being with my children. If I was with my children, I spent most of my time checking my work emails. Regardless of what I was actually supposed to be doing at any given time, my mind was elsewhere or in many places, forever making mental lists. I was constantly available to everyone. I was never available to just myself. I was highly stressed and terribly guilty.

And so I resigned from the job that I loved, that I was great at, and that gave me an enormous amount of self-worth, because I felt I had no choice. I had backed myself into a corner where I believed I could either be a great mom or I could have a great career—but not both.

What on earth had happened to the promise that I could *have it all*? I felt cheated, lied to, robbed, exhausted, set up and a complete failure who, having tried to fly the flag, had in fact dismally let the sisterhood down.

If only I knew then what I know now about *time*, because I made the wrong choice—I didn't need to opt out of something I loved. I had fallen into a couple of massive traps, not least of which included superwoman syndrome, imposter syndrome and paralysis by guilt.

Sound familiar?

About four-and-a-half minutes into being a full-time mom I was climbing the walls.

As a solutions-oriented person, I set about looking for a book with all the answers to how I could better manage my time so that I could be a great mom, have a great career and live a better life. However, the books I found were either full of theory and psychology, or fluff and nonsense; or frankly took up too much of my already over-stretched, precious time just in the reading; or were written by men (I'm sorry boys—but you simply don't get it).

And so, not satisfied with what was available, I redesigned my time myself. Reframing my relationship with time saved me then. And it saved me again years later when my marriage failed and the parenting buck stopped with me. Full stop.

I developed a simple, do-it-myself process that helped me track and rate my time, and analyse what my time habits were costing me; I then implemented a series of simple and sustainable solutions to invest my time smarter. I broke my framework into five distinct steps—and it worked. It worked for me and then it worked for my friends. And so, I built a business around it.

Time is my purpose and my passion. I am a time investment specialist, global speaker, best-selling author and coach. I am in the business of helping you find time. Lots of time. I work with high-performing teams and individuals to teach them the framework, strategies and mindset to maximise their productivity (across all aspects of their lives). My purpose is to help you take your success to the next level and to absolutely ensure that you never, ever, feel that your only option is to choose between two things you love for a want of time.

And I love every minute of it.

Welcome to my gang

You are a clever, savvy, successful woman. But are you being *smart*?

You have a lot of balls in the air and mostly you are happy to let a few drop here and there. But as you progress in your career or as your business grows, it seems that those balls are multiplying exponentially. It is getting harder to keep the balls in the air and the challenge you face is that you may well drop the lot.

You have achieved your success to date with talent and hard work. But these qualities won't take you to the next stage. You need to start doing things differently because your current approach in trying to *do it all* represents the biggest risk to your success. And frankly, you are bleeding time.

I am here to help you reframe your relationship with time. I believe that you are extraordinary. When you gain control of your time you will be unstoppable.

Welcome to my gang.

Kate x

PART I
The mistakes we make — what could get in the way?

In *Me Time* I shared seven common mistakes busy, clever women make when it comes to investing their time well. In *Me First* I have amped this up—there are way more than seven mistakes I see you making, and I want to expose them.

Every mistake is supported with stories from incredible women from around the world so that you know you aren't alone in indulging in some of these crazy habits. I also share proven strategies so that from now on you will be equipped to smash through every single time-sucking roadblock you put in your own way.

Investing your time better is not about being perfect, it's about being smarter. If we didn't make mistakes we would have nothing to learn from or to improve on. However, sometimes we don't learn from our mistakes. Sometimes we fall into the nasty little habit of repeating the same mistakes over and over. And worse, some of the mistakes we continually repeat exacerbate our major pain points, such as not having enough time. Some of our behaviours actually result in us having even less time. Part I of *Me First* is all about these mistakes and the traps to look out for.

Our afflictions

Where we waste our time

It's ridiculous how afflicted we are—we high-achieving women. I am not an expert on these afflictions, but as a former fellow sufferer and now having worked with many of you, I certainly have some pretty strong opinions that I want to share.

From the time we were young girls, we were inundated with a never-ending barrage of subliminal and overt messaging telling us that, as females, not only can we have it all, but we deserve it all. Anything boys can do we can do too—the messaging states—because we are as smart, as brave, as capable and as deserving to win the scholarship, to be the CEO, the managing director, the head surgeon, the partner of the law firm, the next astronaut to orbit the earth, the leader of the country, or the person at the helm. Ostensibly, there are no barriers to what we can achieve because all things being equal, we are equal.

And yet, biology got in the way. We have wombs, you see, which means we are the only ones who can grow and spit out the babies. And from the moment that little sprog takes hold, the messaging suddenly changes. Now, it's not so much, 'You can be the CEO'—it's more, 'How long are you going to take off work?' (*Really!? Just six weeks?! Is that all? But how will you bond with the baby?*); 'Breast is best you know—are you planning to breastfeed your baby?' (*Really? You are going to formula feed? Goodness, is that good for the baby's immune system?*); 'You must be looking forward to having a break from work?' (*Oh, a nanny? I sometimes wonder why some women have children at all!*).

This change in messaging not only confuses us, it is an assault on everything we have been positioned to be and to achieve. It undermines us and immediately puts us on the defensive. We thought we were being judged on our smarts, not our breastfeeding boobs. We thought we were admired for our ability to hold our own around the boardroom table, not our ability to set the dinner table. We were raised for great careers—but along comes a baby and the rules suddenly change.

But let's take this back a step. Because this is all about being a high-achieving woman and what this means in terms of motherhood.

It took me over 12 months to fall pregnant with my first child. It was a time of great sadness and self-doubt for me. It was also the first time in my life that someone held up a mirror and forced me to look at myself in a different light. Just prior to falling pregnant we saw a gynaecologist to start investigating our fertility. The doctor was very clinical and very matter of fact, while I was a blubbering mess. Why could we not get pregnant? What could we do to ensure we got pregnant? What tests? What medicine? How could we access fertility drugs? IVF? She eventually interrupted me: 'This is the reason why I hate working with high-performing women,' she said, 'because you think you can control all of the outcomes. And you can't control this one.' I was speechless. 'Go and book a holiday. Lie in the sun. Relax. Have sex and then if you aren't pregnant in six months come back and see me.' I walked out of her office vowing never to set eyes on her again. How dare she speak to me like that? How dare she judge me? How dare she?

I booked the holiday and promptly fell pregnant two minutes later and spent the entire trip vomiting. But that's an aside. How dare she?

Yes, she was cruel. Yes, she was blunt. Yes, she was cold. But in truth she was also right. I was a high-achieving woman. I was used to success (not by luck, but by lots of bloody hard work), and here was something I could not control through talent, determination or hard work. It was my first brush with the devastating downside of being a high achiever. I was 29.

I don't know about you, but for the entirety of my first pregnancy I focused exclusively on the birth experience. I virtually gave no thought at all beyond how the hell I was supposed to get that thing out of me. And then all of a sudden I had a baby, and it was forever, and I had absolutely no idea what I was doing.

The rules had changed—I was expected to, and was more than happy to, heavily invest my time and energy into my children forever more. My fanny had just been through a nuclear assault, I was stitched up from one end to the other, I had an ice pack in my undies, my boobs were rock hard and leaking, I had cabbage leaves shoved into my damn ugly maternity bra (God knows why, but I was simply doing what I was told at this point), I was covered in sick and poo and I was sleep deprived. I was not trained for the transition from professional woman to motherhood; from fully competent to mostly incompetent; from decisive to indecisive; from being physically and mentally responsible for just me to being fully responsible for me plus one (and then plus two and then plus three).

And so, what did I do? I reverted to the formula that had worked well for me in the past. I did the research and I collected the data. I read every 'how to' book on motherhood and babies that I could lay my hands on. Why? Because I am a high achiever and like everything else that is important to me, I needed to do motherhood really, really well. And then I plastered a smile on my face and I winged it.

The trouble with motherhood, however, is that the rules constantly change. From the moment your baby emerges into the world, you live in a state of constant awareness that you don't have a bloody clue what you are doing. Every single 'milestone' brings new challenges and new issues and new doubts and uncertainties. Just as you think you have a handle on how to deal with a newborn and sleeplessness, they turn one and start walking around poking their fingers into power points. Just as you learn to handle the niceties of preschool, they turn 10 and don't want to kiss you at the school gate. Just when you learn to handle a 13 year old, they turn 16 and want to go to parties and drink alcohol. One day you are buying them nappies and the next you are buying them condoms. There is no systemising these challenges. You can't write up a process or automate motherhood. And so you are permanently winging it. And that is bound to undermine anyone's confidence, let alone a high-achieving woman's.

But there is more to it than this—because as a mother you now also need to rethink and navigate your career through an entirely new lens. There is often an expectation from the men (and let's face it, the women) around you that you will be the primary carer. This was certainly the case for me: both my husband and my male boss expected that I would put my legal career on hold and 'tread water for a while' (the words of my boss). And I was compliant in this. I was the one who did the career sacrificing. My husband earned more than me, it is true, but there was never even any discussion about it. Besides, I wanted to be with my babies. And when my maternity leave finished, I returned to work part time because I wanted to be a present mom and I felt enormous guilt at the thought of my kids being in full-time care. When the children were sick, I was the one who took time off work to care for them. When I moved back to full-time hours, on very good money, this trend continued. In fact, I can count on two fingers the number of times my husband stayed home to care for the kids when they were sick. But let me be clear, this was driven in large part by the fact that I wanted to be the one with my sick children.

I am not a psychologist. I am not trying to analyse this. I am just relaying my lived experience as a working mom, which, by the way, is also the lived experience of most of the working moms I know where both parents work. This is also not about laying blame—it is simply about reporting exactly how it was (and still is) for me. Yes, there was an expectation that I would sacrifice my time and career, and no, my husband did not offer, but there was also a very strong reluctance on my part to give up parenting control.

What other women say

Having kids is really hard when you have a desire to be your best self at work and as a parent. I absolutely love being a Mom and a CEO. I know that I'm good at my job as I put my heart and soul into it. As a CEO I work with my colleagues to ensure our organisation is leading the way in gender equity including being a flexible, agile and family focussed work place. I want future generations of female leaders to have better support and greater opportunities to be present for their families too without the guilt or need for permission. This is how we bring our best selves to work.

Kelly Grigsby, CEO, Wyndham City

Having a child did not change my skill set, but it did change my (former) employer's mindset. Despite my wins, I did not feel valued. I did not fit in as a 'mom'. They made it very clear that they wanted to employ young women who weren't going to have kids.

Angie Weston, Executive National Vice President, Arbonne

I personally felt that I only had the capacity to manage one child. This meant that there was only one child to leave when I went to work, and therefore only one lot of guilt.

Rebecca Casson, CEO, Master Builders of Victoria

While motherhood has been the greatest achievement of my life, it has also been the greatest source of guilt, self-doubt, anxiety, imposter syndrome, superwoman syndrome and judgement.

So, what does any of this have to do with time? Everything. Because somewhere along the journey from professional woman, to mom, to professional woman and mom, you moved from the driver's seat in your life to the passenger seat. And it's time to take back control—by changing your relationship with time.

This is not a time management book. This is a time investment book. From today on, your time is not something that needs to be *managed*. Just like your money, your time is a precious, limited resource that needs to be wisely and consciously *invested* for the greatest possible return. Once you shift your mindset from one where you *manage* your time, to one where you only ever *invest* your time in exactly the right tasks at exactly the right time, you will move from being a reactive participant in your life to being the active, in-control, central character who gets to curate your life and your experiences for maximum success. It's exciting!

There are two ways to waste time. You can waste it:

- on time-wasting thoughts
- on time-wasting tasks.

Some or all of the time-wasting thoughts/mistakes below will resonate with you. It might feel uncomfortable to read these home truths, but be courageous: if you recognise yourself as making any of the following mistakes, put a big star next to the mistake, or dog-ear the page. Acceptance is the first step to making the changes you need to make.

Let's deal with the waste-of-time syndromes first, before moving on to the rest!

Mistake #1

Imposter syndrome

You have been faking it, big time. You really have no idea what you are doing. And it is only a matter of time before someone comes up and taps you on the shoulder and quietly asks you to leave the room without making a scene.

Research is quite clear that imposter syndrome is more common in high achievers. Of course it is. As if we didn't have enough to think about. Outwardly, we have all the trappings of success, but we are not able to internalise our successes. Our internal dialogue is one of self-doubt.

Social media—that glorious online world only a tap away where everyone, *every*one, is perfect—does not help. But that's the point: they are perfect because their profiles are stylised to be perfect. There is a significant lack of authenticity on social platforms. You do realise, don't you, that you are comparing yourself to something that isn't even real? Was there ever a greater waste of your time?

I have literally been winging motherhood from the day I found out I was pregnant 21 years ago. Am I a good mom? Will my kids have friends? Will my kids do drugs? Will my kids be good at sport? Will anyone play with them? Am I present enough? Are they happy? Am I setting the right boundaries? Am I a mom or a friend? Do other people think I'm a good mom? Do my kids think I'm a good mom? Am I a good mom?

There was a period of my life as a mom where hours of my time were spent with my kids in the emergency department at the local hospital. I think there were seven broken bones in all—one of my sons had three broken arms before he was three years old. Aside from the breaks, my kids are also literally glued together. On one memorable day I had two separate trips to the hospital for my oldest, and then my youngest, to have them both get stitched up after different accidents. The triage nurses knew my name. I genuinely thought family services might come calling. Is it any wonder I regularly contemplated whether I was actually any good at being a mom?

Motherhood is a massive part of our lives, and because we spend so much time second guessing ourselves in our capacity as moms, it should come as no surprise that feelings of self-doubt start to creep into other aspects of our lives. And then we start to question our abilities professionally: Am I any good at this? Do I deserve to be in this role? Do I know enough? Am I good enough? What if I am asked something I don't know the answer to? Am I going to fail? At any moment now is it all going to come unstuck and people will realise that I am a fraud?

What other women say

I thank God for all those years I spent in amateur theatre as a child! I have often felt like I am faking it. I'm in my 40s and for the first time in my career I don't feel like an imposter. The more exposed I am to others the more I realise that I do have the credentials and the experience. I used to reflect on my achievements and find a way to diminish them – am I good 'enough'? Over time I have recognised the impact I am making.

Kelly Grigsby

I used to say *no* to certain industry invitations because I felt like I did not know enough to be in the room. But I eventually realised that I don't have to know it all — certainly no-one else in the room knows it all. My mentors have mentors.

Julie McDonald, CFO, MDH Pty Ltd

I don't think I've ever really known what I am doing. I think I've always just kind of used a bit of intuition and a bit of intelligence and a whole lot of grit to make things happen. I completely feel inadequate most of the time.

Alexandra Depledge, Founder, RESI

I have felt like an imposter not only around men but also other women. The stereotypical female executive — impeccably dressed, high heels, great hair and makeup — is just not me.

Tracey Slatter, Managing Director, Barwon Water

I have lived with imposter syndrome for a long time. Even when I found myself selected for the polar medicine unit as a solo doctor in Antarctica I still felt there had been a mistake!

Dr Meg McKeown, Antarctic Medical Practitioner, Australian Antarctic Division

I have absolutely experienced imposter syndrome. Like many women, I think I'm my harshest critic, and sometimes see what's left to do, or what could be improved, more easily than what's already right.

Amy Henry, President, FlashLight Insights

Self-doubt can be limiting when it comes to managing your 'today', but when it threatens your capacity to explore wonderful new opportunities 'tomorrow', then it is unforgivable. No-one ever said on their death bed: 'I'm so happy that I left those opportunities on the table because I did not think I was good enough.' Every single one of us needs to wing it from time to time. I certainly do. But just because we might have a few less-than-entirely-authentic moments, does not mean that we are living a completely false existence.

It's time to back yourself—you *do* know enough and you *are* good enough.

Solution

If and when you are seized by imposter syndrome, remember these simple truths:

- This is not about being inauthentic; it's actually about developing a new skill—the skill of backing yourself and your ability to get stuff done on the run. Start saying *Yes I can* instead of *No I can't*; start saying *Yes I am* instead of *No I'm not*. This is your new mantra—say it again and again until you start to believe it.

- Imposter syndrome is a feeling, not a fact—get the data before you go too far down that rabbit hole. Make a list of your achievements, your successes, your qualifications, your wins big and small and genuinely reflect on them. Every time you start to doubt yourself, get your list out and read it.

- When opportunities arise that you think you are unworthy of, remember that if you say *no*, someone else will be lining up (potentially someone less worthy than you) and they will have the guts to say *yes*. They will jump and then build the parachute on the way down and you will look on and think, *That could have been me*. Stop coming second. It's time to be first.

- Connect with other incredible women, share your self-doubts, share your wins and get them to do the same — a little bit of group validation never hurt anyone.

- Talk to yourself the way you would talk to your daughter or best friend when she shares with you her feelings of inadequacy or self-doubt.

- Know that one day, maybe when you are 40 or 50 or older, you will wake up to the realisation that you actually have been good enough all along; that you do know what you are talking about; that you are an expert or specialist in your field; that you do add value; that you don't need validation from anyone else to make this so; and that there is nothing to fear. So why not own it now?

- Never forget: we all wing it.

You are a high achiever for a reason. Don't waste any more time being anything less. Take a deep breath, get over it and jump.

What other women say

I see mothers experiencing imposter syndrome and I always urge them to reflect on the current project they are undertaking (motherhood) with no manual or performance review. The skills you acquire as a mother are undoubtedly transferable, and make mothers more than qualified to command a boardroom.

Christine Michel Carter, Mompreneur and Me

Looking back at the last three years I can see I've come a long way but when I don't write it down at the time, it's easy to forget what's been achieved.

Caroline Jean-Baptiste, Superstar Mortgage Broker and Owner of Mortgage Choice

Mistake #2
Busy lifestyle syndrome

You know how the conversation goes when you catch up with your friends:

> **Hey! How are you?**
>
> **Oh, I'm so busy! How are you?**
>
> **I'm busy too!**

And then you spend five minutes talking about how busy you are and how busy everyone in your life is and wouldn't it be great to not be so busy and to have a bit more time.

'Busy' seems to have acquired significant social status: it gives you membership to the 'Busy Club', which brings with it all sorts of awesome member benefits including a declaration to the world that you are very, very important. You have lots on your plate, lots of people wanting a piece of you, lots of projects on the go, lots of work, lots of clients and lots of places you need to be. It allows you to feel busy, to look busy and to talk a lot about being busy.

And yet, is the 'Busy Club' really one you want to be affiliated with? Just what is it you are actually doing all day that has generated all of this busyness? Aside from the fact that you probably don't know what it is you do all day, every day, have you ever thought about how you sound when you talk about how 'busy' you are? Because every single time you say 'I'm so busy!', what you are actually saying is 'I'm so unproductive!'

What other women say

You wouldn't believe how many times I've had to stop myself saying the word 'busy' since I met Kate Christie!

Julie McDonald

Busy is overused. Anyone can be busy with low-value activities: it is a way to keep yourself occupied. I don't need to be occupied; I need to be productive.

Caroline Jean-Baptiste

Some people seem to think, 'The busier I am, the more important I am.' You see this, for example, with barristers: they will rarely say 'I'm quiet'. Busy is a meaningless word.

Carmel Mulhern, Group General Counsel & Group Executive Governance, Commonwealth Bank of Australia

Busyness is not a badge of honour, and it's time to call it for what it is: a boiling frog. Now, without having conducted the experiment myself, essentially the story goes that if you put a frog in a pot of boiling water it will immediately jump out; however, if you place the frog in cold water and slowly raise the temperature, the frog won't perceive the danger and will slowly cook. The boiling frog is a useful metaphor for our inability to react to threats that slowly sneak up on us—like the feeling of overwhelming busyness. It's not like you can pinpoint the day you became 'busy'. And yet, like the frog, you are slowly cooking your brain.

Scottish researchers have coined a new disease to describe this human condition: BLS, or Busy Lifestyle Syndrome. I kid you not.

Solution

If and when you suffer from busy lifestyle syndrome, try these strategies:

- Remove the word 'busy' from your vocabulary and substitute it with something else: 'I'm terrific!'; 'I'm so productive!'; 'I am moving at pace!'
- Get the data: until you know exactly what it is you do all day that is creating this sense of overwhelm, you can't know what changes you can make to your habits and your time investment. Step 2—Map—of The 5 SMART Steps will show you how to do this (see part II).

What other women say

I don't consider 'busy' a negative word. It's just the manner in which I often live my life.

Kate Jenkins, Sex Discrimination Commissioner, Australian Human Rights Commission

I understand the stigma around the word 'busy', but for me it's a practical word that really reflects the flow of my days. I don't use it to impress anyone. As a single mom to two little boys and working, life is 'busy'.

Lucy Kippist, Editor, Flying Solo

I am trying to embrace the moments when I don't have a day filled with 'to-dos', and the courage to tell people, 'I'm not busy this week' — and that's okay; it's not a sign of failure.

Jane Hall, Founder and Principal Lawyer, Loupe

Mistake #3
Superwoman syndrome

What do you think of her? You know who I mean. She is poised, relaxed, in complete control of her successful business or career, all without compromising her home life. She has more freedom than you. She has more time than you. She has more energy, less guilt, less stress and greater happiness. And she looks amazing. How is it that her children always look like they have just stepped from the pages of a magazine when you are lucky if you can get your kids to leave the house with shoes on?

Closely associated with imposter syndrome, you may also be suffering from superwoman syndrome. The pressure we feel to do it all, and be it all for everyone else, is staggering. Best mom, best career woman, best wife, best daughter, best business owner, best basketball coach, best cake maker, best boardroom presenter, best leader, best mentor, best counsellor, best crazy woman. Other women seem to be able to do, have and be it all, so surely you can too? And maybe if you just keep going, at pace, it will all work out, and while the wheels might be wobbling, it's all good! And I can fit in a jog too. And I need to make sure the kids are eating good, healthy food. And I need to take the car in for a service. And I need to help my son write his speech. And I need to walk the dogs. Just keep going, just keep going. I'm fine. I'm fine. Really—I'm fine!

She truly seems to *have it all*. She is unfazed, unruffled and, quite frankly, unbelievable. What is she doing that you aren't? What is she doing that you can't? How the hell does she do it?

What other women say

I had a picture on Instagram with a celebrity and someone responded: 'I want your job! I want your life!' But that is not my job. There are a lot of people who see a couple of cool moments and they think this is all you do. And that's a misconception. But I guess it wouldn't make interesting Instagram to post meetings or checking stock at the warehouse all day.

Maria Hatzistefanis, Founder and CEO, Rodial

I focus on being the best version of myself and what's important to me.

Snezana Jankulovski, Chief People Officer, CyberCX

Of course, in the deep recesses of my mind or moments of insecurity I have compared myself to other women. But I pull myself up sharp when I do — that other woman might appear to 'have it all' but just like me, she will be struggling.

Alexandra Depledge

Solution

If and when you find yourself afflicted by superwoman syndrome, remember:

- A little bit of healthy competition never hurt anyone. Identify that person a rank or two (or five) higher than you and in a positive way use them as a role model to strive to improve yourself. After all, this is what we do every single time we identify a mentor we want to work with.
- However, a lot of comparison or negative comparison where you aren't actually looking to build up your skills and capacity, but rather to diminish and criticise yourself, is not healthy.
- Stop thinking 'she' is doing a better job than you. She is not.

- Stop second guessing your own actions based on your perception of how someone else lives her life. You have no idea what she is going through, how she feels, or what she is juggling and struggling with.
- Many of the women you are comparing yourself with are full of the same self-doubt as they look at you and wonder how you do it all. Ironic, yes?
- Stop chasing her dreams. Set your own goals. Identify your own values. Live your own life and do it a whole lot smarter and with greater happiness and confidence than you are right now.

What other women say

Comparisons never take you to a good place. When people in my cohort do well I feel buoyed by their success rather than threatened by it.

Sarah Wood, CEO, Unruly

For me, this isn't about living up to an outside view of what a supermom might be, but rather using my energy in ways that give me purpose and meaning.

Amy Henry

Women who compare themselves to other women are normal. If women can recognise the energy, style and determination of others and wonder what drives them, it's fabulous.

Kate Halfpenny, Entertainment and Lifestyle Editor, The New Daily

I like to be inspired by other women but not compare myself to them. We are all diverse with different contexts, challenges, ambitions and styles.

Tracey Slatter

(continued)

What other women say (*cont'd*)

I think it's normal to compare yourself to others, and often when I do, it's to get inspiration and courage to be the best person I can be.

Kate Jenkins

It's good to have both female and male role models that you compare yourself to and that you aspire to be like. I don't think of it as a negative, I think it is a positive.

Carmel Mulhern

Mistake #4

Yes syndrome

If you are continually saying *yes* to all the opportunities that come your way, then three things will happen:

1. You will quickly run out of time.
2. You will continue to put yourself last (which means you are actually saying *no* to yourself).
3. The requests will keep coming as you are a renowned *go-to girl* who always says *yes* and who always delivers.

There are two types of opportunities:

1. Those which require your time investment right now; for example, 'Can I have five minutes of your time right now?'.
2. Those which require your time investment in the future.

The vast majority of opportunities that come your way fall into the latter category: they are future-facing opportunities that require you to commit today without the actual pain of spending your time today. You are committing to spending your time in the future, which makes for an easier *yes* (because it does not hurt right now!). This is a big trap: how often do you reflect back on that decision and think, *It seemed like a good idea at the time, but what on earth was I thinking?*

And just what were you thinking?

What other women say

I have a filter for the requests I receive: (i) Does it interest me? (ii) Can I add value? (iii) Will I be able to give my best? (iv) Does it fit with my family?

Janine Allis, Founder and Managing Director, Boost Juice (Retail Zoo)

(continued)

What other women say (*cont'd*)

I have trouble saying 'No' because it's my nature to want to help. I try to work out what is really needed from the request and if I can facilitate the person getting what they need in another way, I will do that.

Carmel Mulhern

Often it's 'no' now but that doesn't mean it can't be a 'yes' in the future.

Snezana Jankulovski

I often reply to a request with, 'Can I get back to you?', so I can stall a little and work out if it is something I really want to do. However, I also preface the 'No' with an apology, which I need to work on.

Lucy Kippist

You don't have to do absolutely everything. You can actually say, 'I'm not going to do that.'

Joy Foster, Founder and Managing Director, TechPixies

Solution

If and when yes syndrome affects you, keep in mind that your time is money, which means you need to have both a financial budget and a time budget.

Your financial budget is a set amount of money you can invest at home or at work over the next 12 months for the greatest return for you and your family or for your team. You can't overspend against your financial budget because once the money runs out, you are in the red. If there are competing opportunities, products or services you want to invest your money in, you need to weigh up the advantages and disadvantages and allocate your limited resources wisely.

Your time budget also needs to be invested wisely for the greatest possible return over the next 12 months. Like your financial budget, there is a cap on your time budget, and you can't overspend. If you get close to overspending, then you need to constantly reassess your choices to determine what is a good/necessary time investment and what needs to be taken out of the budget as a poor/unnecessary time investment. This way, instead of thinking that you have to say yes or no to each opportunity that comes your way, the question is really one of: *Do I want to invest my time or do I need to decline?*

THE DO'S

Make sure you *do*:

- have a very clear idea about your values—exactly where do you want to invest your time?
- ask yourself, *Is this really the best use of my time?* If not, that's a good indication that you should decline an opportunity
- hear the person out before you jump in with an offer that means committing your time. They might just be letting off steam or about to tell you they need to reschedule something you had planned. Hold your tongue and let them finish
- think about whether there is an alternate way you can help the person without committing time from your time budget
- buy yourself some time to genuinely assess the opportunity so that you don't rush into a decision that you later regret. Use a response such as, *'Thank you for thinking of me. Let me check my calendar and I will come back to you'*. Or, here's a unique alternative: tell the truth! When someone asks for a favour which you don't really want to do, be honest. Try: *'I can't score the basketball on Saturday because I just want to watch my son play this week'*. Or offer an alternative that is a win:win: *'I think I am scoring next week. Do you want to swap?'*

- be sure to pick your mark: if the opportunity comes from your boss or your kids or your mom, a great strategy is to respond along the lines of, '*I am currently working on x, y, z. If I also take this task on, then one of those other tasks is going to slip. How do you want me to prioritise these tasks?*'
- practise declining—like any new skill you are looking to adopt, you need to invest time in honing this skill.

If all else fails you, my fail-safe go-to when I decline is, '*Thank you for thinking of me. I am working to a deadline at the moment, but if anything changes I will come back to you.*' Let's break this sentence down:

- *Thank you for thinking of me*: it's polite and it conveys to the requester that I am grateful for the opportunity
- *I am working to a deadline at the moment*: these words, at least in my world, seems to terrify people and they will nod understandingly while backing away
- *but if anything changes*: leaves the door open for me to change my mind later
- *I will come back to you*: stops the requester chasing me any further.

THE DON'TS

Make sure you *don't*:

- worry that people might like you less if you decline an opportunity. If you lose some friends, maybe they were not the right people to have around you in the first place.
- feel the need to apologise for making decisions about where you do and do not invest your time—really, it's no-one else's business!
- confuse problem solving with the need to take on endless amounts of work. It's all about prioritising, delegating and rejecting—all of which we will get to in part II.

What other women say

I say 'No' in a straight-up way but with a dose of sugar: 'Thank you for the lovely opportunity, but it's not the right fit at the moment. Hope it's a terrific success.'

Kate Halfpenny

Sometimes saying 'No' means giving someone else in my team the opportunity to participate in something amazing.

Carmel Mulhern

It's imperative to know what your limitations are, and when to say 'No', or sometimes 'not now'. The key is to offer an alternative solution or interim guidance until I have time to become more heavily involved.

Jane Hall

Sometimes the opportunity is so great you have to say 'yes'. If the 'yes' is to the right opportunity, you can create your own future.

Angie Weston

Mistake #5
Judgement

People will judge you, and often that judgement hurts. And, in my experience, as high achievers we tend to focus on the negative, or not-so-good, comments and not the amazing and oh-so-good comments. I used to be terrible at this. At a speaking engagement, if 99 people rated my talk as excellent and one person rated my talk as good, I would focus on that one person: *Why was I only 'good'? What did they not like? Where did I go wrong? Should I have ...?*

What a waste of time and energy. Why did I not celebrate the 99?

I wasn't always like this. B.C. (Before Children) I was much more resilient, and much less inclined to worry about unfounded judgement (or let's face it, even founded judgement). A.C. (After Children), however, I was consumed by this whole baby world where I felt completely out of my depth most of the time and my self-confidence took a dip. I found that I was dialling down the value I placed on my own voice and judgement, while dialling up my preparedness to let the voices of others undermine my decisions. And that permeated from baby world to the rest of my world.

Add to that the fact that everyone—and I mean *everyone*—has an opinion on how you should be mothering, and you, my friends, are on a hiding to nothing.

I remember one father expressing his surprise at my going back to work after I had my second son. He asked me what I was going to do with the kids (mind you, what was *I* going to do—not what was *my husband* going to do ...) and I told him I was working part time and my boys would go to daycare three days a week. 'Did you know,' he said, 'studies show that kids who go to daycare from an early age are more likely to suffer from anxiety and depression?' Terrific, thank you for your support.

I was racked with guilt (see mistake #6 on page 32). The whole time I was not with my babies I thought about them and worried that I was damaging them. One day I turned up at daycare to collect the boys and my second son was sitting on the floor crying. No-one was comforting him and the emotion I felt at seeing him was quite literally physical—it was like I had been punched in the stomach. I rushed into the room, swept him up, turned on the carer and demanded to know what was going on. I was furious and she was flustered and defensive and I don't blame her in any way for saying, 'What you need to understand is that your son is a very unhappy little boy.'

What other women say

In my 20s and 30s, juggling two full-time jobs—motherhood and journalism—I put my hand up for everything so nobody could say I wasn't there for my children. I wanted to appear perfect, and it was a lot of pressure. I wish I could go back and tell that woman not to worry about baking a cake at 10 pm and to just stick the kids on the train with wrinkled uniforms.

Kate Halfpenny

I used to work through lunch just so I could leave work on time to pick my daughter up from care. I was made to feel so guilty every time I left that building: 'Oh! Are you leaving now? Have you got something to get to?!'

Angie Weston

I'm acutely aware that we are all struggling with something we don't wear emblazoned across our chest for the world to see: 'Divorced Single Mom 2016'; 'Widow 2013'; 'Unwell Child 2020'. You cannot and should not judge when you don't know the facts.

Julie McDonald

Judgement happens to all of us as working mothers. So many people I have come across in my career cannot believe that I am a mom as well as a CEO. They cannot understand how I

(continued)

What other women say (*cont'd*)

can do both: 'Oh my goodness, you have a child!?' It is still very much a gendered thing.

Kelly Grigsby

As a teenager, I told my mom about a girl who had fallen pregnant and adopted the baby out. We were Catholics and the 'no sex before marriage' mantra was drilled into us. I was so confused when, rather than condemn the girl, Mom said, 'It can happen to anyone.' Twenty years later I discovered it had happened to my mom. Judgement is a game we all must play with caution.

Caroline Jean-Baptiste

The saying that women have to be twice as good often applies. Women are expected to execute their roles flawlessly and often take on other roles — team builder, mentor, advocate, counsellor, and maybe even party planner — that men are not burdened with.

Amy Henry

Solution — judgement

Let's address this nonsense once and for all. There are no winners in the judgement game.

- If you are a mom and work full time, people will judge you. If you are a mom and work part time, people will judge you. If you are a mom and don't work, people will judge you. If you are exactly like them, they will judge you. If you are different from them, they will judge you. You are literally damned if you do and damned if you don't. And so I urge you not to give a damn at all.

- Live your life the way that works best for you. Make the choices that work best for your family and for you. Wear a coat of mirrors so that you reflect back to people the judgement they seem to want to inflict onto you. And bottom line—as hard as it can be to accept—their opinion of you is absolutely none of your business. Stop wasting your precious energy and time worrying about their judgement. Not my circus, not my monkey.
- You can't control what people think of you or say about you or to you, but you absolutely can control how much time and energy you invest in worrying about what they say.

Never forget:

- You have worked extremely hard for your success.
- You are really, really good at what you do.
- You are an incredible role model for your daughters and for your sons.
- There are plenty of women and men around you who are immensely proud of everything you have done and continue to do to make it all work for you and your family.
- Yes you have made sacrifices and yes there have been trade-offs, and that is what being a strong, amazing woman is all about.

Hence this is an intervention. Every time you catch a sideways look in your direction, pursed lips of disapproval or even open criticism about the choices you are making as to where you invest your time, or don't invest your time, come back and read this section again. And then, again.

What other women say

Judgement makes me furious. I believe you have to pull other women up behind you. The problem is that many women say this and then I see them not doing it.

Alexandra Depledge

If what I am doing is right for my business or my family, the people who judge are just background noise, and to be completely truthful, actually add a little motivation to work harder and do even better.

Nicole Pennefather, Owner/Director, Get Franked

Women should support and encourage each other; we have enough of a challenge as it is.

Snezana Jankulovski

If you have time to judge others then to me it seems that you are not yet comfortable in yourself.

Lucy Kippist

I work in a very male-dominated industry and some people have mistaken one of my male colleagues as the CEO; shaking his hand and not mine. Some men also say things to me that I suspect they would never say to a male CEO. For example, at an event one man said to me, 'Oh, did you drive here all by yourself?' I replied 'Yes I did. It has been legal for women to drive in this country for many years!'

Rebecca Casson

Solution — feedback

Be careful not to confuse judgement with feedback.

I categorise judgement as advice that is not well-intended; and feedback as advice that might be hard to hear, but where there is a positive intention by the giver to help you grow.

Never forget:

- Judgement can wound, whereas feedback is a gift.
- If you disagree with feedback that comes from someone you care about or respect, take the time to ask them on what evidence they reached their conclusion. This could be a valuable moment for a lesson.
- Focus on the lesson, not the person. When someone takes the time to provide you with constructive feedback, even if it is hard to hear, always thank them. They have gone out of their way to help you because they want you to get even better, and often their insights are invaluable.

What other women say

Have an amazing community of non-judgemental colleagues from across the world who are willing to help you or listen to you.

Anu Acharya, CEO, Mapmygenome

I have never been judged in a professional sense – well, not that I have been aware of or have given energy to. I honestly have not ever contemplated it. Maybe I have been judged? It is interesting to reflect on; it's not an attractive characteristic.

Carmel Mulhern

I'm very careful not to judge other women as we already come under so much more scrutiny than men and are usually our own worst critics, so the last thing we need is to start judging each other! When women build supportive networks and champion each other it can make a huge difference to combating unconscious biases in the workplace.

Sarah Wood

Maybe I have been judged, I haven't really noticed. You can't change what other people think of you. But you do have a choice: you can dwell on it or you can choose not to care.

Janine Allis

Mistake #6
Guilt

My oldest child was eight months old when I fell pregnant again. Having agonised for months trying to fall pregnant the first time, it seems we had hit upon the recipe for success the second time around a little quicker than I had anticipated. And so I was already pregnant when I returned to work part time. My best-laid plans for the career and baby juggle were already out the window, and within a few short months of returning to work I was back on maternity leave.

I felt enormous pressure to return to work earlier than I really wanted after my second baby. The anguish of leaving that little baby at daycare was almost debilitating. Part of the guilt was because I wanted to continue breastfeeding. I had fed my first son for 12 months and I could not get past the fact that if I was to feed my second son any less than 12 months, I would somehow affect his future or health, or in some way (God knows how) he might feel that I loved him less. And so, here is what I used to do: every day I would leave work at midday and drive back to the daycare to feed him, and then put him to bed at daycare and dash home to continue working remotely from the office, before collecting him and his brother in the afternoon. I did that every single work day for four months, until I could tick off that I fed him for a full 12 months.

Why do we do these things to ourselves?

Our job is to protect, love and nourish our babies. But was it really meant to be this hard? Every day as moms we are forced to make decisions, and some of them impact our kids, but absolutely every single one of them impacts us.

What other women say

If a mother says she hasn't felt mother's guilt, she's lying! It's certainly been a big part of my life.

Julie McDonald

Two weeks after I returned to work from maternity leave, I left for a buying trip to New York, and I missed my daughter's first birthday. It was horrendous. It took me a decade to get over that guilt. Being a mom had everything to do with why I left my job to start my business: the six-figure salary simply wasn't worth what I was missing out on.

Angie Weston

For most of my career I have struggled with mother's guilt: Am I available enough? It's always there in the back of my mind. I think guilt is pretty unique to mothers. We have this need to be a 'good mom' at the same time as being effective in our career and I don't think men experience this, or not to the same level. It's only now that my daughter is almost an adult that I feel confident I have set a very strong example for her.

Kelly Grigsby

As my children get older, and I hear them talk about the importance of hard work, commitment, and passion for what you do, I feel a little less guilty and a little more proud of my choices.

Amy Henry

Sometimes I feel self-indulgent for the decisions I make, such as having a massage instead of spending time with my family. The guilt is always there.

Rebecca Casson

Solution

Here's what you need to understand:

- It's time for some tough love: get over yourself. Seriously. Do you honestly think you would have been happy, or happier, or a better mom, or even remotely fulfilled by opting out of such a crucial part of your identity (your career) to only nourish part of yourself (being a mom)?

- Your guilt is getting in the way and frankly, it is a waste of your time.

Here's how you're going to achieve this solution:

- Part II will help you reframe your day. You will find at least 30 hours of lost time a month, which is time you can invest in what is most important to you (including quality time with your children). You will adopt new behaviours and take new actions to change your overall environment for the better.
- You will also examine very closely where you are currently investing your time and you will see that you already do a lot with and for your kids. Some of this 'doing' is about to change—and trust me, guilt does not have a part to play in reframing your time.

What other women say

Don't do guilt. It's an emotion that sucks up energy, time and confidence.

Sarah Wood

The best thing about having a great career was that when my kids were at school I had something to nourish and challenge me. I would have gone mad otherwise. There would have been way too much time to wonder why I had worked so hard only to find myself in a life where exercise classes with a girlfriend were the best part of my day.

Kate Halfpenny

I'm the mother other women hang out with to make themselves feel good about their parenting! But I threw guilt away. It gets down to what is most important to my kids. If they really want me there, then I will be there.

Janine Allis

I used to feel guilty about being at work and not with my daughters, and then guilty when I was with them and not supporting the business. Now I don't feel either. I like to tell myself that my daughters are seeing a strong woman going to work and being a role model, still while feeling loved and cherished.

Alexandra Depledge

When my kids were younger I always worked. I had my business and that never stopped. I really worried about how they would grow because I wasn't around them that much and we always had help to take them to school. I really worried whether I would connect with them and would they like me. Now they are older and I see kids whose mothers stopped work to raise their kids and I see no difference. I didn't know that then. But now I'm okay.

Maria Hatzistefanis

Mistake #7

It's easier if I just do it myself

When you start implementing The SMART 5 Steps (which you'll find in part II) much of what you used to do around the house for everyone else and which you have promised yourself (and me) that you will no longer do, will be lying around on the floor simply begging you to deal with it. And you might be tempted to revert back to doing it all yourself because: *It's easier; It will save a fight; You feel that you should; You really don't mind doing it; It only takes 5 minutes; You are better at it; It really is your job after all; and blah, blah, blah* ... Sorry, I stopped listening to you at *It's easier.*

Solution

Keep in mind that while it is important to have a really good to-do list, it is just as important to have a really good don't-do list. Old habits die hard; however, they will die. The solutions for mistake #7 are in part II.

Mistake #8
My kids aren't going to make this easy

You are about to implement some massive changes to how you invest your time. Your kids will not take these changes lying down (even though lying down often seems to be their preferred position when it comes to helping around the house). They will not be cheering you on from the sidelines in your campaign to invest your time the SMART way. On the contrary, they will be actively working against you, because your changes mean pain for them. They have suddenly been evicted from the executive floor of the hotel. They will be shocked and annoyed at having lost access to their personal maid service (a.k.a. *you*) and they will come out fighting.

Give them some credit. Your kids are not stupid—they will try every trick in the book in an attempt to wear you down. They will whinge, complain, argue and talk back. They will compliment you as being better at the chores than them. They will explain that they are too busy to do their chores because you told them to do their homework. They will tell you they have done their chores when they have not. They will pretend they don't know how to do their chores. They will disappear.

It's your turn to prove that you are not stupid.

My kids, like all kids, are master manipulators. When my oldest son was about 10, I added changing their bed linen to the kids' chores. I remember dressing it up as an awesome opportunity:

'This is so great – you get to choose the doona cover you want!'

My son was initially enthusiastic, which lasted exactly one change of linen. The next time the task came around, this is exactly how it played out:

> **'Oh mom, can you do it for me because you are soooo much better at making beds than me.'**

And he looked at me with his big puppy dog eyes and my heart just melted.

> **'Okay, honey. 'Come with me and I'll make it for you.'**

He sat on his brother's bed and I made that bed up so beautifully that it could have been on the front cover of a bedding magazine. When I finished changing the linen, he smiled at me and said,

> **'See mom, I told you that you are better at it than me.'**

> **'Yes, but that's because I have had lots of practice. So, now it's your turn.'**

And I undid the lot, handed him the sheets and sat on his brother's bed to watch.

Solution

You need to stay ahead of the game.

The solutions for mistake #8 are in part II.

Mistake #9

My partner is the problem!

And then there is your partner. It is quite possible that your partner is your oldest child and will not take these changes lying down either.

Solution

If you think your partner is the problem, remember that implementing and benefitting from the changes you are about to make will be much easier if you have your partner's buy-in. Get your partner to read *Me First*: they might learn something (but maybe pull out the insourcing section on page 139, where I share how to manipulate your partner ...). Take the pressure off yourself by discussing with your partner the changes you want to make and, more importantly, how you as an individual, how you as a couple, and how you as a family, will benefit from the new arrangements (the exact solution for this is expanded on in part II).

Mistake #10

I was told I could have it all. What happened?

Work/life balance is a myth. You cannot perfectly balance all of the many facets of your life by giving equal time to them. Work is simply part of your life. Your family is another part of your life. Your community work, or spiritual pursuits, and volunteering efforts are other parts of your life. You live one life and balance does not come into the equation.

Solution

If you thought you could have it all, remember:

- You might think that you can have it all. You might even think you need it all. Wrong. You don't actually need to have it all—you only need to aim to have all the bits that are most important to you. Stop setting the bar so high. Just focus on what is most important to you and forget the rest—it's just a distraction.
- Shift your mindset away from one of work/life balance to one of work/life integration—where you give yourself permission to spend your time where it is most needed at any given time. If it is with the kids, then focus on the kids. If it is at work, then focus on work. Explain this philosophy to your kids: that you will be there when you can and when it is most important and when they most need you, and

then stop bashing yourself up for every single time-based decision you make.

- This is about being the best version of you. Overcoming mistake #10 is what *Me First* is all about!

What other women say

You can have it all, but only with the right support network. If you don't have the right support, it is impossible to make it work.

Alexandra Depledge

It is always tempting to try and 'do it all', but you don't have to do it all yourself! You need to learn to value your own time.

Angie Weston

I am asked to do a lot of amazing things that in the moment I really want to do. But the reality is I don't have the time or energy to do everything that sounds enticing.

Kate Jenkins

Mistake #11

I don't need help

Not asking for help when it's needed goes hand in hand with having *yes* syndrome. It's a double affliction—always saying *yes* to everyone else but never asking for help when you need it.

Trying to do it all by yourself while attempting to maintain and grow your success is not sustainable. Your physical and mental health and happiness could be impacted. Your relationships could be impacted. Your sense of self-worth could be impacted. Your productivity and successful career or business could be impacted.

These are significant risks.

Look at this through a different lens: if you do get to the point of burnout, in your absence you will be replaced by a team of people who will manage the many facets of your life until you get better. So, if it takes a team of people to replace you, how is it that you thought you could manage to do it all on your own in the first place?

Solution

If you think you don't need help, remember that it's okay to ask for help. It's okay to expect help. It's okay to pay for help. Start seeking help when you need it. Overcoming mistake #11 is addressed in part II.

What other women say

I have a global health business and five children and the only person I didn't know how to look after was me, and that is so typical of women. And I remember getting super, super ill and being on a drip in hospital and thinking: 'Oh my God, if I die, my ex will have to look after the kids.'

Geeta Sidhu-Robb, CEO, Nosh Detox

My employer provided me with a private room for expressing after I had my first baby; they paid for my husband and baby to fly around the country with me so I could get on with my job without compromising my role as a mom; and they promoted me to Group COO when I was pregnant with my second child. It's still a juggle, but when you are 100% supported as a mother at work, it makes a world of difference".

Jane Tandy, Chief Operating Officer,
Canaccord Genuity Patersons Limited

The gender divide is still so great — women still do the lion's share of parenting and there is often an expectation that we will. But I'm also an executive, which means I burn the candle at both ends. And all of that means that I put myself last and I always have.

Kelly Grigsby

Mistake #12
I just don't know where to start

You know you need to invest your time smarter, but you have 1000 excuses as to why today is not the best day to start. Today you are too busy, too tired, too unmotivated. Whatever.

There is never going to be a best day to start investing your time smarter. But you do need to pick a day. I know you are 'busy' (see mistake #2), so assuming you allow yourself two weeks to read *Me First* and to complete all the exercises, you can confidently circle a Monday at 9 am three weeks from today and lock this deadline into your calendar: 'From today I *invest* my time the smart way.'

If you don't commit and lock in a deadline, then you will be defeated by the economic theory called Parkinson's Law, which essentially provides that: *A task expands to fill the time made available for it.* You know how Parkinson's Law works: if you have a month to complete a report, it will take you a month to complete the report. If you have three days to complete a report, it will take you three days to complete the report. If your eight year old has two weeks to build the paper mache volcano and forgets to tell you, it will take you and your eight year old two hours to build the volcano the night before it is due (and it will certainly look like it was built the night before). That's Parkinson's Law. You know this to be true.

Solution

If you're not sure where to start, embrace Parkinson's Law and set a deadline in your calendar to change your mindset from one of time management to one of time investment.

Mistake #13

I don't have time for me

Moms birth the babies, and as such we face a millennia of both biological and societal pressures to nurture our children and to put their needs first. Someone has to do it, right?

Until the 1960s it was relatively common for western countries to have a marriage bar, whereby women were required to resign from their employment when they married. Regardless of the rationale or fairness of the bar, one outcome was that those women who could (and chose to) have children, could devote their time—full time—to being mothers and carers for their family.

But, happily, times have changed. We are no longer required to forego a career in order to catch a husband. How blessed we are.

And yet, as a woman who is a mom and who also works, I cannot help but regard that woman of the pre-1960s with some degree of envy. Not because I don't want to work—trust me, I do. But simply because what that woman had that we do not, was the ability to look forward to and to enjoy some guilt-free time for herself. Because at some point in time she knew her children would go to sleep, or go to pre-school, or go to kinder, or go to school, or go to high school, or go to university, or go to work, and she could have some time to, and for, herself.

But what of women who juggle motherhood and paid employment? When is our down time? When do we ever switch off?

We can celebrate the human rights, women's rights and notions of equality that have advanced us significantly since the 1960s, allowing us more choice as women, but I for one am not about to applaud our failure to demand a different parenting and workplace construct to support our status as women who work and who are also moms.

We are killing ourselves with an epidemic of selflessness. We never put our own needs first. We rarely carve out time for ourselves. And when we suddenly do find ourselves with a little bit of spare time, what do we do? We fill it with another task that has nothing at all to do with enjoying Me Time, and which has everything to do with doing something for someone else.

The whole point of *Me First* is to get you back at least 30 hours of lost time a month to live the life you really want. A life that is a little less self-less.

Solution

Remember that:

- The 5 SMART Steps work (see part II)
- this process will work for you
- it's time to put yourself first.

What other women say

I am worthy of putting myself first.

Ali Villani, Author

With my first business, there was five years of blood, sweat and tears … and hair apparently. I cut my hair and my hairdresser said: 'Joy, do you know you have a bald spot?' I had lost my hair from the stress.

Joy Foster

I don't wish I had more time, but I do wish I had less things to do in the time that I have.

Carmel Mulhern

We are the first generation of women creating the lifestyles that we are living. So many of us are female breadwinners and that is not necessarily something we were brought up to do. I was definitely brought up to stay married, look pretty, without being deeply intelligent, and to stand quietly in the corner. We are breadwinners, we are boundary pushers, we are boundary creators, and it is taking its toll on us.

Geeta Sidhu-Robb

* * *

Some or all of the mistakes in part I will have resonated with you, so next time you catch yourself walking along the path of darkness, pause, rethink what you are doing and change your course. I will explore this further in part II and offer more solutions and more time investment tips.

PART II
The 5 SMART Steps

Part II is a deep dive into your personal time habits. We will work together through The 5 SMART Steps to find you 30 hours plus of lost time a month. There are a series of exercises in each step that will help you reframe forever your relationship with time. Bottom line: you are here to transition from 'Everyone Else First' to 'Me First'.

All about Alice

I'd like to introduce you to Alice, your companion to getting back 30 plus hours a month to live a life that you completely curate for yourself. This is all about moving from a reactive to an active mindset. Alice was introduced to my readers in my first book, *Me Time*, and she resonated big time.

You will be able to read over Alice's shoulder as she works her way through The 5 SMART Steps. My intention is that you will draw inspiration from Alice's progress, along with a few ideas on what you can do differently for yourself. Alice is your case study, but she is also a little lifebuoy that you can cling to when you feel like you might be going under.

The wonderful thing about Alice is her complete honesty. While you might be tempted to fudge the data in some of the exercises, you can rest assured that Alice will be airing all of her dirty laundry. Hopefully this will encourage you to also let your guard down. If Alice can let it all hang out, then so can you. Remember: no-one is looking at what you write down.

It is amazing to me how many women have told me that they felt like I had a hidden camera in their house to get my inspiration for Alice. Alice isn't a real person; she is an amalgamation of a lot of different women I know, including lots of me. I think Alice is in all of us.

You may not love Alice—she can be a bit cheeky and self-deprecating—but (as I say to my kids when they are hating on me) she's your guide, not your friend. Despite this, you might see a bit of yourself in Alice, so feel free to laugh at her (after all, you will just be laughing at yourself).

Alice

I am Alice. Thirty-eight years old. Senior associate knocking on the door of partnership with a global consultancy firm. Two children: Henry aged 11 and Olive aged 9. Happily married, mostly, to John (who sometimes masquerades as my third child – which technically speaking would make him my first born).

We have a healthy combined income, live in a beautiful house in our suburb of choice, two cars, a gym membership that I don't use, a dog, a cat, three chickens, not enough time with the kids and no time for each other. I like the dog. I hate the cat.

At work I am held up as a role model and mentor for the young female talent that the partners are terrified of losing. It's all about having a good gender balance, you see, and I seem to be the mascot. 'See,' they say to the young female recruits as they point to me, 'you *can* have it all – a successful career, a beautiful family and all the trappings of success – just look at Alice.' Smile, Alice. Smile.

If only they knew.

In reality I am literally just holding it together. I work full time in a well-paid job that I love. I also work an infinite number of hours a week for no money at all as a mom (a job I also love – I just wish it paid more). I am all things to all people: mom, cook, cleaner, washer woman, shopper, taxi driver, teacher, nurse, counsellor, basketball coach (don't ask), football team manager (don't ask), wife, lover (which to be honest I am often too tired for . . .), accountant, advisor, mentor, manager, friend, daughter, sister . . .

'Multitasking' is my middle name. I am perfectly adept at dropping into the supermarket each day and grabbing just what we need for that night and not a bean more, mobile pressed to my ear with one hand, pushing the trolley with the other, while steering with my hip. No-one can run faster in heels than me when it comes to dashing for my car to get from the city to the kids at school, while making a mental 'to-do' list of everything I need to do tonight, tomorrow and the next day. I am a whirlwind as I vacuum the floor, feed the pets, check my emails, make dinner for the family, help with homework, check my emails, listen to John's day (I really don't care; I just nod and make soothing noises) and then collapse into bed and check my emails.

Awesome. Just awesome.

I am being pulled in so many different directions that I fear one day my arms, legs and head will simply pop off and my torso will be set upon by all those who want a piece of me.

Sure, I might look like I have it all. I sure as hell do it all. But enough is enough. Despite appearances, I don't have it all. I don't even want it all. I certainly no longer want to do it all. I am not loving this life that seems to be happening to me. I am calling it for what it is: my name is Alice and I need more time.

Please.

The 5 SMART Steps: an overview

In the past few years, I have absolutely shifted my focus from one of time management to one of time investment. Somewhere along the way it became very clear to me that we cannot, and should not, try to 'manage' our time.

Apart from anything else, when people talk about time 'management' it always seems to be in a negative context: 'I am so bad at managing my time', or 'I need to manage my time better'. More important, however, is the fact that time genuinely cannot be managed. Not in the same way that other things—such as your health, your diet, your team and your thoughts—can be managed. All of these can be 'managed' to the extent that they can be planned, organised and controlled (and in this context, certainly time could also be managed if the concept of 'managed' ended there). But 'manage' also denotes something that can be 'directed' or 'commanded': your people, for example, can be 'directed' by you giving orders to them. Your health can be 'directed' by you following a strict diet. Time, on the other hand, cannot be 'directed' or 'commanded'. And this is where the term 'time management' falls short: no-one—no matter how smart, savvy, wealthy or stealthy they are—can change time, acquire more time, turn back time, speed up time, or in any other way 'direct' or 'command' time to do what you want it to do. Time marches on, regardless.

And so, I have shifted my mindset to one of time investment—SMART time investment to be exact. This is an important mindset shift that I also want you to make, because it means that you are consciously elevating time to a higher status: just like your money, time is a limited and precious resource that must be invested consciously and wisely for the greatest possible return.

The 5 SMART Steps, which I first introduced in 2014, is a proven framework that will help you track, rate and cost your time, and then set up a series of simple and sustainable solutions to invest your time smarter. You will work through a series of logical exercises to gather the data on your personal poor time habits and challenges, and you will apply your own critical analysis to this with a view to taking control of your time.

Sounds easy, right? Well, no. If it was that easy you would have taken control already. You need to commit to doing the work. The 5 SMART Steps is not a slapdash quick-fix: there is rigour and you will find yourself being challenged as you assess and analyse your current time habits, then reframe and finally implement new time habits.

Just like investing your money to make more money over time, if you invest the time now to get this right, you will make more time—much more time—in the future. So, shift your gaze from the window and let's get started with an overview of The 5 SMART Steps.

Step 1: Self-aware

Having absolute clarity over what drives you is central to deciding where you should, and should not, invest your time. The first step of The 5 SMART Steps is to be self-aware. Ironically, the reason we rarely take the time to reflect on things like, 'How do I feel about this life I lead; the people I engage with; the time I devote to my family, friends, community, spiritual and volunteering commitments; and so on?' is because we simply don't have the time.

In step 1 you will identify your:

- *key time challenges*—what keeps tripping you up, getting in the way and robbing you of time?
- *values*—what is most important to you; where do you want to invest your time?

You'll identify your challenges and values so that you have a baseline against which to reflect on your current time habits and against which to measure the improved behaviours you are about to implement. You also want a very clear understanding of what you are, and are not, prepared to sacrifice your time for.

Step 2: Map

Your day is made up of a multitude of competing demands on your time. So, how do you know which time investment is the best?

To make the right decisions, you need the data: Where do you spend your time? What habits or rituals do you engage in and when? How often are you interrupted? By whom? Do you procrastinate? Are you easily distracted? Is there a pattern to the interruptions and distractions? How often are you on your device? How often are you off your device? How many emails do you receive? How many meetings do you have?

You cannot fully respond to these types of questions about your daily time usage without a full set of real-time data. Besides, once you see the data, you will have a clear idea of exactly how much time you waste, which is a great motivator for change.

Step 2 involves mapping one to three days of your time, preferably two work days and one weekend day. It's a personal time audit to clearly identify exactly where you currently invest your time from the moment you get up to the moment you go to bed: everything you do for yourself, your kids and your partner; every call; every email; every interruption; and everything else that makes up the cacophony of your day.

You absolutely need this data because you can't know what changes you can make to your time investment habits until you know in detail exactly where you spend your time.

Your mapped time will provide you with an incredible amount of valuable data that you will dissect in the following steps.

Step 3: Analyse

Step 3 of The 5 SMART Steps gets you to analyse your tasks and allocate each of them to one of the following categories:

- *musts:* the tasks that you, and only you, can perform
- *wants:* the tasks that you undertake just for yourself—the fun stuff
- *delegate:* the tasks that someone else can perform for you in return for payment (or for free)
- *reject:* the tasks you don't need to do at all, or that you do need to do but which can be done smarter, faster or differently.

SMART time investment is all about getting rid of the low-value tasks (Delegate) and the no-value tasks (Reject) to make time for what you really want to do—the fun stuff (Wants)—and to focus your attention on the tasks that generate your income (Musts).

The delegate and reject categories are where all the gold of your lost time is buried—this is where you will find and harness hours of lost time.

Step 4: Reframe

Step 4 is decision time. You will take all the data you have collected and then decide exactly what you are going to delegate and reject, and exactly what you are going to invest your time in (Musts and Wants).

Step 5: Take Control

Step 5 is all about implementation, momentum and sustaining your success. The 5 SMART Steps is an iterative process. Like a summer detox program, the idea is to revisit the framework at least annually to recalibrate your personal time investment habits. Over time, some poor habits may slip back in; or you will want to reject and delegate other tasks because now you know these tasks are not the best use of your time; or your circumstances may change, which will require you to reflect on your career, life goals and values, and adjust.

The secret 6th step: the power of collaboration

Your first instinct might be to put up the shutters and deal with transforming your time all on your own. However, don't underestimate the power of collaboration.

If you decide you need some additional help or if you think you will get your best results by working with others, then tap into your personal network and collaborate on working through the framework.

You have a lot of people around you who know how you tick, who have a point of view on your strengths and weaknesses, and the changes you might need to make to invest your time smarter. So grab a group of friends, read *Me First* together and tap into their rich vein of advice.

Alice

I can't believe I forgot to take cookies for the school stall. And now it's too late to dash to the supermarket to buy a packet because everyone saw me turn up empty-handed and they will know I *cheated* (and then maybe they will realise that I cheated last time too ...).

Who comes up with these ideas anyway? Why do we need to have a school stall to raise money for 'iguanas in danger'? I don't care about iguanas. Who knew they were in danger? Why the extra pressure? Honestly, it would be easier if I just wrote the school a cheque for $200.

Why can't I remember these things? I know why: because I have 10 bazillion things chasing each other around my head.

I don't know what's worse: the look of disappointment on Olive's face, the looks of pity on the other moms' faces or the teacher's pursed lips. When Sarah offered to share her 'home-made' muffins with Olive could the ground not have opened up and swallowed me whole?

Damn, damn, damn.

Can't you just teach my child to read, write and count? You have one job: am I asking too much here? Is testing the agility and ability of the mother and then holding her up to the scrutiny of the school community now on the curriculum too?

Bad mom. Bad mom. Bad mom.

Stress and guilt. Love it. I just wish I had more time. More head space.

Imagine if I found those 30 hours a month. Ohhh ... But, can I park my guilt and need to be perfect long enough to do this? I know the way I think: even if I get back hours of time, I will probably just feel tormented over how I should spend that time. I will probably ... Damn it, Alice! Just get over it. Time is money and it's time to put my money where my mouth is.

Okay. Let's go baby.

Step 1
Self-aware

The first step to getting back genuine quality time requires some self-reflection.

Alice

Am I self-aware? How do I feel? Is this really necessary? Where do I start …? Can I lie down for this?

It's 10 pm. I need a wine. God I'm tired. Oh dear, now John wants to talk about his day. Maybe if I just sit here and quietly sip my wine and nod every now and then and make noises like 'oh, yes, aha, yep, no' he will think I'm listening.

I have to remember to set my alarm for 6 am so I can make the school lunches before I head out to my breakfast meeting. I'm going to wear my white dress. I can wear it with my black shoes; that always looks hot to trot. Put phone on charger. Oh damn it, Henry has assembly tomorrow. I promised him I would go. I'll call Mom in the morning to see if she can go and watch. I can't believe that email, I need to get onto that first thing. Roast chicken for dinner tomorrow. I can pick up the chook after my lunch meeting. Henry has footy training and Olive has dance (argggghhh); I might be able to share drop-off and pick-up with Suzi. Maybe I can watch football training to make up for missing assembly?

(continued)

Alice (*cont'd*)

'Yes, honey, I agree.'

Need cat food and milk. God I hate that cat. Cereal. Dry cleaning. House looks like a bomb has gone off. If I leave the dishes until tomorrow, hopefully someone else will do them. Yeah, right. Interstate next week for two days; check with Mom to do those days for me. Or maybe John can do them? Yeah, right. I need to catch up with the team tomorrow and set up that new internet protocol. Damn, I forgot to call Henry's teacher back; I hope it's nothing bad.

'Honey, I just remembered Henry's teacher called. Can you call her tomorrow? Plus, don't forget you are on school drop-off tomorrow. Yes, I did tell you. I told you on Tuesday. Yes I did. I told you I have a breakfast meeting. Yes, I did!'

'For God's sake, John, I can't do it all!'

You are 'busy'. You have so many balls in the air that it's only a matter of time before you start dropping a few. You are trying your best to get everything done and (mostly) you do it all (fairly) well.

It's hard.

When it comes to investing your time, and keeping all those balls in the air, most successful women will have some key time pain points that challenge them again and again. And yet, have you given much thought to what these key time pain points are or how you can fix them?

As a busy woman, self-reflection is not something you often do. Ironically, it's partly because you don't have the time, but it's also because a healthy session of self-reflection can be pretty confronting. Too bad. It's time to walk into the room of mirrors and take a good, hard look to see how you actually feel about this life you are living.

> **What other women say**
>
> Self-reflection is really hard!
>
> **Rebecca Casson**

There are four exercises below and their purpose is to give you the head space for a little self-reflection.

Exercise 1: my key time challenges

You need to know the time challenges that constantly get in your way and trip you up. By having these front of mind as you work through The 5 SMART Steps, you will be mindful of the habits and behaviours you need to change. At this point, don't worry about finding solutions (that comes later). For now, it's all about awareness.

Having surveyed thousands of high performers, I have found that there are a number of time pain points that come up again and again:

- I am constantly interrupted (59 per cent of people surveyed identify this as their number one pain point)
- I don't have enough time (40 per cent of people surveyed identify this as their second highest pain point).

And then, in no apparent order:

- I have too many competing priorities.
- My day is a constant juggle.
- The emails never stop.
- I have back-to-back meetings.
- Delegation does not work—I may as well do it myself.

- I waste too much time.
- I am easily distracted.
- I find it hard to say *no*.
- I have no time for myself.
- Travel/commuting is killing me!

Circle any of these that resonate with you, and jot down any other key time challenges you have.

What other women say

My main challenge is the extensive amount of travel I do, which means I am away from my family and my team more than I'd like, and the travel time can disrupt my productivity.

Kate Jenkins

1. I always end up doing too many things at once, even though I know it makes me ineffective. 2. I keep my phone on silent, but still end up checking it repeatedly. 3. My brain doesn't really kick into gear until I'm scared, so the real work doesn't happen 'til the last minute.

Claire Hooper, Australian Comedian/Writer/Presenter

Exercise: due to juggling a family and a senior executive position, I have to either go to the gym at 5 am or very late after work. This means some days I don't get home until 8 pm, which doesn't leave a lot of time for family and down time.

Snezana Jankulovski

Being present with my son when I am with him is my greatest challenge. I hate it when I get home and connect with him and a call comes in that I have to take. It feels like I am sending him a message that he comes second.

Tracey Slatter

Finding time to see my parents: it's important to me because I know we don't have all the time in the world left, but I don't do it often enough. My ideal would be to do paid work four days a week and spend one weekday with Mom and Dad.

Kate Halfpenny

That's a good start. Now, let's dig a little deeper.

Exercise 2: how do I feel right now?

Answer each of the questions below with *yes* or *no*. Work quickly through the questions and trust your first instinct. Next, reflect on each answer and jot down a few reasons why you gave the answer:

1 Am I stress free?

----

2 Am I guilt free?

----

3 Am I happy?

----

4 Am I calm?

----

5 Do I have enough time?

----

6 Am I energised?

----

7 Am I healthy?

----

8 Am I fit?

----

9 Do I feel in control of my life?

----

10 Am I focused?

----

11 Am I content?

----

12 Do I have healthy relationships?

----

13 Is my business/career going well?

----

14 Do I spend enough time on myself?

----

15 Am I able to live in the moment?

Unless you have answered *yes* to most of the above questions, you know it's time to make some changes. If your response rate is leaning towards the *no*'s, these are the feelings you want to shift to *yes* by the end of *Me First*.

Alice

Being completely honest here, I would say that I have way more than three time challenges. In fact, I would say I have a list of 'top-25' time challenges. Pretty much every one of those mentioned above, plus a few more. Try throwing in frustration, anger, fatigue, temper tantrums (mine).

Righto, here are the three that I guess are my biggest pain points:

1. I don't have enough time. Ever.
2. I'm constantly guilty about the amount of time I spend at work at the expense of my kids.
3. I'm too tired to change how I manage my time.

How do I feel? Well …

1. No, of course I'm not stress free. I have too much on my plate. Sometimes I wake up in the middle of the night in a stress-induced insomniac sweat. Or maybe I'm just peri-menopausal? Really? Already? Focus Alice. I am not stressFREE, I am stressFULL.
2. No – aren't all working moms guilt-ridden? I don't do enough with my kids. I do nothing with my husband. I never see my friends. I hardly see my parents. I feel guilty leaving work before the 'non moms'. If there is something to feel guilty about, I will find it. I was born guilty.
3. Yes – I am happy when I am at work and it is going well. I am happy when I have quality time with the family. But I feel a level of dissatisfaction with the way I am living my life. On the whole, 'mostly happy' sums me up.
4. No – I am not calm. I yell. A lot. I get angry. John drives me crazy when he doesn't pick up the slack. Then I feel guilty for resenting him. And I don't communicate this; then it builds up and I blow. Big time.
5. Do I have enough time? Are you serious? Of course not. I'm a bloody busy woman juggling a full-time career, two kids, a house, a husband, a dog, a cat, a holiday to plan, dishes to do, dinners to cook, lunches to make and 1000 other responsibilities. Jeez.

6 No — I am tired all the time. I wake up tired. I could do with a nap right now.
7 No — I am fit but not healthy. I drink too much alcohol — sometimes I just watch that clock tick towards 6 pm so that I can open a bottle of wine. I'm tired. I'm stressed. I'm a little anxious. I'd like to be healthier.
8 Yes — I am fit. Jogging is the one thing I do for me.
9 Yes and no — I don't think I'm in control of my life. The thing is, I am great at responding to things that are thrown my way, but to be honest that just means I am dancing to someone else's agenda. But I do have choices available to me. If I was truly unhappy or felt like control had completely slipped over to the dark side, I guess I would make other choices? On the whole, not as much control as I'd like.
10 No — when I'm in the work zone I'm definitely focused. The rest of the time I am anything but focused. I would describe myself as manic.
11 Yes — I am content. I have a great job, awesome kids, I love John. My family are healthy. I am just so tired. And I would like more time. But I am content — life could obviously be a lot worse.
12 Yes — I think my relationships are healthy. I know I need to learn to switch off and focus when I am with the kids. I need more one-on-one time with John. When was the last time we had a conversation that didn't involve coordinating our schedules? I neglect my friends. And my parents.
13 Yes — career all good. Love it. Flying. Just guilty because I feel less than successful at home. Failure is probably too strong a word, isn't it?
14 No — probably not enough time on me. I squeeze in 3 x 30-minute jogs a week.
15 Do I spend time in the moment? Sorry — what did you say? Bahahaha …

Oh dear, 6 out of 15. Not ideal. Ho hum.

Exercise 3: what one thing would I change?

Review your answers to the above questions, have a think about your comments and then answer these questions:

1. How do my comments make me feel?

----

2. If I could fix one of the pain points from exercise 2, which one would I choose, and why?

Alice

1 How do my comments make me feel?

Not great. I really need to make some changes. It's actually pretty bloody depressing, self-reflecting. But, in a weird way it's funny too. Funny that I have just been zooming along so fast that I haven't taken the time to sit down and think about my life. About whether I am happy, content, calm, enjoying myself. I haven't asked myself these questions before. Ever. And now that I have, I feel like I have opened Pandora's box.

2 If I could fix one of the above, which would I choose, and why?

I choose *more time*! Thinking this through and reflecting on my answers, not having enough time really seems to be the root of all of my other pain points. If I had more time, I could spend some of it on my kids, which would reduce how guilty I feel. And I could reorganise my life, put myself first from time to time, and maybe get back some energy. And if I had more time I could lose that sensation of always rushing from one thing to the next, chasing my goddamned

> tail to get it all done. And if I had more time I could sit in the sun for an hour on the weekend drinking a gin and tonic while reading that book that has been sitting on my bedside table for two years. And ... yes, more time would be nice.

WELL, NOW YOU KNOW

This is not all doom and gloom. I don't want you to look at your responses, admit defeat and curl up into a small ball under your chair. It's okay to admit you are not (currently) living the dream. The whole idea of self-reflecting as the first step is so you know where you are at, right now: draw a line in the sand and commit to this being your starting point. When you finish The 5 SMART Steps and have secured your 30 plus hours of time back a month—time to prioritise you—you can look back to see how far you have come!

This is good. Breathe.

You can see that change is needed. Give yourself permission to make that change. Understand and agree that you do not need to be a superwoman. Understand and agree that if you don't at least tweak your time investment habits you will not be the best person you can be, and getting to the next level of success in your career or business will be much harder to achieve and sustain. You will continue to be under-productive. You will continue to be unhappy, or stressed, or guilty, or angry or whatever the feelings are that you have identified above.

WHAT I REALLY, REALLY WANT

As a highly successful woman you are driven, you work hard, and you love the buzz of each win you achieve. There is a lot of upside to this. The downside, however, is that it can be hard to flick the switch to *Off* to invest some of your time on things that aren't work related. For good or bad, work is often your drug of choice. And when you do have time, well, that tends to be spent on anything and anyone other than yourself.

However, as you are about to get back hours of genuine quality time to live the life you really want, wouldn't it be nice to spend some of your reclaimed time on pursuits other than work? Let's make this real with a list of activities you want to invest some Me Time in as you start reclaiming your lost time. Some of you will have a ready-made mental Wants List a foot long. But if not, and if it has simply been too long since you put yourself first, then the following broad categories might assist:

- Me First—just me, me, me and no-one else
- Family and friends
- Personal growth or further education
- Physical, emotional, mental or spiritual health
- Growing my career or business
- Investigating a side hustle.

It's time to put yourself first. This is all about prioritising you.

What other women say

I wish time would stop every now and then so I can just catch up with my life; and I wish my kids would stop growing up so fast.

Kate Jenkins

You need to do something outside of work and family and your business. Just for you. Carve it out of your diary and do it. For me, it's roller derby. Create time for yourself or you will go insane. It's so important to give back to yourself.

Nicola Moras, Online Visibility Expert

Exercise 4: what will I do with 30 extra hours a month?

At this stage of The 5 SMART Steps, the primary function of your Wants List is to remind you that you are now on a very simple, exciting mission to get back 30 plus hours of lost time a month. It's there to motivate you and help you maintain momentum in working through the rest of The 5 SMART Steps.

Start your list below. If you are having trouble coming up with ideas (if it has simply been so damn long since you did anything just for you), then think about your closest friends who are also moms, but who seem to make time for themselves. What do they spend Me Time on? Think about their hobbies, interests, pursuits, classes, sports, what they do with their friends, what they do with their kids, what they do with their partners and what they do as a family. If any of the activities resonate with you, then add it to your own Wants List.

What other women say

I schedule what I value, and I turn up. I value health so I schedule workouts in the mornings.

Caroline Jean-Baptiste

Between the age of 30 and 40, I was growing my business. Consequently I had no friends and little Me Time. I had my business, my husband and my kids. It had to be that way. Now, well, Me Time for me is on a yoga mat, hanging out with friends (I have friends now!), sitting on a beach, surfing, playing with horses.

Janine Allis

I go to the gym six days a week because it makes me happy and it gives me energy. I schedule 'time for reflection' into my day, every day from 8 am to 8.10 am where I spend 10 minutes visualising what I am doing that day, where my business is going, and to reflect on what is most important to me. This keeps me motivated.

Angie Weston

My Wants List:

Alice

My Wants List:

- Take up boxing.
- Learn to meditate and then practise every day.
- Do a barista course.
- Teach the kids to cook without yelling at them.
- Hit the shops with a vengeance and update my wardrobe.
- Jog more regularly.
- Get a lover (just kidding, John — I thought you might be snooping ...)
- Plan a family holiday.

Take a copy of your Wants List and put it on your fridge, next to your computer, behind the toilet door—or anywhere you spend a bit of time thinking. We will come back to this in step 4—Reframe.

What floats your boat?

Your Wants List will also help reveal what is most important to you: it is closely aligned to your values. And when it comes to investing your time well, your values are key.

Your values are what you stand for: the principles, beliefs and moral compass that guide your decisions, including how you choose to invest your time. They help you identify what is most important to you so you can establish your priorities, focus your time and effort and stop chasing the shiny objects.

You will have many values, most of which will remain consistent throughout your life and some of which will change depending on what is happening of significance to and around you. Knowing which of your values are the most important to you will help ensure you make the right time-based decisions. You don't have time to do everything, so it makes sense to focus on what is most important to you—and articulating your values will give you absolute clarity over where you do, and do not, want to invest your time.

So, what are your values?

This answer will be different for every single woman who reads *Me First*. It's your life, your family and your career or business, so don't look at 'her' and wonder what floats her boat.

Defining your values

Have you ever thought about what is most important to you?

Genuinely reflecting on your core values can be confronting—but none of this is about judgement. It is all about understanding yourself and your drivers. If, for example, your automatic response is that 'family time' is your most important value and yet you work around the clock, travel for work and rarely see your family, then you are either kidding yourself (your top-most value is more closely associated with success at work—which is absolutely fine) or you are living with terrible guilt because your work/life choices are not aligned to your values.

So what drives you?

What other women say

Fear used to be a huge component of what drove me. I had everything on the line. It was the fear of failure. The fear I would be caught out as not knowing what I was doing. It was almost debilitating. I would forward project and plan for every possible outcome. The upside was that we never ran out of money, and I could deal with most challenges that came my way because I had planned for them!

Janine Allis

My values are key to deciding where I want to spend my time and when. If there is a conflict, I assess where the greatest need is.

Julie McDonald

For me, being successful is number one. That means I need to look after myself both physically and mentally, so I prioritise going to the gym, eating well, and learning and developing.

Snezana Jankulovski

I had not really reflected on my values before. When I did, I realised that my core value is optimism, and everything else is driven from there. I always try my best in everything I do, and if I don't get it right, then my second most important value kicks in: resilience.

Rebecca Casson

I have done a lot of work on my values over the years and my hard-core, non-negotiable values, in order, are:

1 *family:* spending quality time with my kids. If my kids need me or want me (and often if they don't) I will be there—rain, hail or shine. I will be there if I have to travel across the country; or across the world; or be up at the crack of dawn; or in the middle of the night; or if I need to get up from my sick bed. It's a straight-up ***yes***. I did actually get out of bed, sick with the flu, to take my daughter to her first rock concert—we were in the mosh

pit, everyone was sweating from dancing while I was sweating from my fever, but I was not going to miss it, or mess it up for her, no matter what, and it was ACE.

2. ***business growth/success:*** spending quality time on my business—if it is an opportunity for my business, then it's another *yes.*
3. ***my health and wellbeing:*** I am the first to admit that in the past I have not consistently prioritised Me First in this space, mostly because I got so caught up in numbers 1 and 2. But I reframed this space last year—you can read more about how I did that in step 4—Reframe.

Despite my values articulated above, I think that it is really important to acknowledge that there have been many times in my working life where I have prioritised work over my kids. Often this has worked out okay and there have been no consequences. But there have been times when it did not work out okay, and that stays with you. When my son was in his first year at school and I was working as a corporate high flyer, I was invited to a compulsory weekend retreat for executives from my company. I was new to the executive team and this weekend was a big deal. There was no question of me not going. My son wasn't feeling well and was crying and wanted me to stay with him. I remember driving away from the house with my son standing, watching the car—I could see him in the rear-view mirror and my heart was breaking. The next evening my husband called to tell me my son was sick. Really sick. I fretted all night and got the earliest flight home in the morning. I made a doctor's appointment from the airport, rushed home and collected him: he was so little and so hot and so quiet. He didn't want to be touched and all I wanted to do was hold him. They called an ambulance from the doctor's rooms and he spent four days in hospital with pneumonia. I did not leave his side. The guilt has stayed with me. I completely made the wrong decision to leave him, and that one still stings.

What other women say

You can't do it all. As Unruly grew into a global business I became acutely aware of this, and the importance of mindful prioritisation. There was time to be with my family, be with the children, make sure that I'm a good mom – and then there was time to grow the business. But there wasn't much left over for anything beyond those two priorities (especially as I always prioritised seven to eight hours' sleep a night). It wasn't a problem, though, because it was the path I had actively chosen – I love nothing more than the joy that comes with family time and the intellectual challenge that comes from growing a global business!

Sarah Wood

A lot of people don't understand the work that it takes to grow a business. It's a lot of work. It's really important – something has to give. You can't have everything. So very early on I decided I'm not going to have a social life. It's going to be my family and it's going to be my work. Before I had kids I would go out with my girlfriends and go for lunches and teas, but I just don't have time right now – it has to be family or work and nothing else. It's a trade-off you make. And I'm okay with that.

Maria Hatzistefanis

There are three exercises that follow that will help you identify and rank your values. Be honest. Your answers are unique to you—it doesn't matter what anyone else thinks—this isn't a competition over who is the best mom or best career woman or best entrepreneur or who has the best values.

When I first undertook these exercises years ago for myself, I had a lot of what I personally call 'vanilla' values—that is, values which I think hold true for many of us: honesty, integrity, success, being well regarded. Don't get me wrong: these values are important and manifest to our sense of being. However, they aren't integral to how and where I want to invest my time. They simply dictate the way I go about my business.

I want you to undertake these exercises from the perspective of identifying your absolute non-negotiable values: if you were lying in bed feeling terribly sick, what would you actually get out of bed for?

EXERCISE 1: WHAT'S MOST IMPORTANT TO ME?

To help identify your values—what is most important to you—complete the following sentences with as many examples/ answers as you like:

I am happiest when …

I love talking about …

My absolute non-negotiables are …

I love to be complimented on …

If I was sick, I would get out of bed for …

Next to each response, jot down the descriptive term that you think best describes/sums up your answers. For example, if you wrote, 'I love playing board games with my kids' (said no-one ever…) you could say that this means you are 'family-oriented'. If you wrote 'being fit and healthy and full of energy' you could say that this means you are 'health-conscious'. If you need help with the descriptive terms, refer to this list:

adventurous, ambitious, assertive, balanced, brave, calm, caring, committed, community-minded, compassionate, competitive, consistent, contented, cooperative, courageous, creative, curious, dependable, determined, diligent, discreet, efficient, empathetic, enthusiastic, ethical, expert, fair, faithful, family-oriented, financially secure, fit, focused, frugal, fun, generous, giving, good, happy, hard-working, healthy, helpful, honest, independent, [of] integrity, intelligent, just, kind, knowledgeable, loved, loving, loyal, original, patient, positive, powerful, practical, private, professional, prudent, reliable, resilient, resourceful, respected, responsible, self-controlled, selfless, self-reliant, sensitive, spiritual, spontaneous, strategic, strong, successful, supportive, talented, team-oriented, thoughtful, trustworthy, understanding, unique, valiant, virtuous, visionary, well-regarded, wise.

What other women say

It was so interesting, reflecting on my values. My family is most important. Time for myself comes last. My professional responsibilities and caring for and helping my team are in the middle. This probably needs more reflection from me. I keep putting myself last, except for small periods of time after holidays when I return to work with a mindset of putting myself first more often, but inevitably that falls away. I need to be held accountable for looking after myself!

Carmel Mulhern

Let's have a look at how Alice went about completing exercise 1.

Alice

Think deeply, be honest, hone this, because it is important to get it right.

1. I am happiest when ...
   - I am jogging (fit, healthy, independent)
   - I win a new client at work (independent, successful, professional)
   - the kids are happy and don't fight (family-oriented, caring)
   - I go on a date night with John (family-oriented, loving, loved).
2. I love talking about ...
   - my work (successful, financially secure, ethical, of integrity)
   - my kids (family-oriented, competitive)
   - good restaurants and nice wine (hungry, fun, curious)
   - who is having an affair (snort!) (naughty!).
3. My non-negotiables are ...
   - good food and nutrition (fit, healthy, food-loving)
   - success at work (ambitious, expert, successful, financially secure)
   - being challenged at work (competitive, expert, honest, talented)
   - quality time with my kids (caring, family-oriented, loving, loved)
   - family birthdays (caring, family-oriented, loving, loved)
   - work deadlines (respected, dependable, hard-working, of integrity)
   - my family's health (caring, family-oriented, healthy, loving, loved).

(continued)

Alice (*cont'd*)

4 I love to be complimented on ...
   - being a great mom (selfless? an imposter?)
   - being a great role model (respected, professional)
   - being a great friend (caring, loving)
   - being really smart and strategic! (expert, successful, talented)
   - looking hot (deluded? hahaha!).

5 If I was sick, I would get out of bed for ...
   - my children, John or my parents (family-oriented).

EXERCISE 2: MY TOP VALUES

Based on the values you identified in exercise 1, reduce your list down to your six to eight most important values. This can be challenging, so take your time.

Based on my story earlier about the time my son ended up in hospital with pneumonia, it was easy enough to judge myself in retrospect. Sometimes we get it wrong.

But this and other guilt trips like it helped inform my true values, which in turn helped me make some really important decisions about my career.

My desire to be with my kids and prioritise them (coupled with the guilt I felt when I got this wrong) while still ensuring that I could have a fulfilling and challenging work life, is what ultimately drove my decision to leave the corporate world and start my own business. Now I am the boss. I set the hours I work. I choose. I am in control—and this control has removed a vast amount of guilt. I get to completely, or almost completely, work around my kids. And this works for me. Starting my own business was 100 per cent driven by my core values.

I continue to reflect on my values regularly, just to check in and recalibrate, so I know I am only ever investing my time where I value it most.

Alice

Damn it, I have too many. How am I supposed to get it down to six to eight? Who knew I was so values-oriented?

But really, who am I kidding? I'm not fun. Do I value fun? I'd like to be fun, but I don't have the time. Okay. Lose fun. Loving and loved — both are important to me, but I guess loving is more important. Lose loved. In terms of work, I have ambitious, professional, successful, hard-working, expert, dependable, respected and talented. I can see a common thread here. Having success is more important to me than having ambition — I am ambitious, but I think the desire for success drives me harder than pure ambition. Lose ambitious; same for talented.

Dependable makes me sound like I'm a Labrador. Lose hard-working — that's just a given. Lose deluded, naughty, an imposter, food loving and hungry — they were a joke ... sort of. Lose self-less: I'm hardly a saint.

Okay, getting there. Bloody hell. This is hard. Clearly 'decisive' is not one of my values.

Loving is stronger than caring to me. Lose caring. Is it cheating to combine 'fit' and 'healthy'? No, I don't think that's cheating, and given I picked 'honest' and 'of integrity', clearly I would not cheat. Ha! I think being of integrity incorporates 'honest'. This is crazy. I will come back to this tomorrow ...

Righto. I'm back. Heeeeere's ALICE! I am focused (oh crud, does that mean I have to add one? No, focused is not a core value, just a state of mind for right now). Here is where I am:

> **adventurous, curious, successful, professional, competitive, independent, ethical, of integrity, family-oriented, expert, financially secure, respected, fit & healthy, loving.**

(continued)

Alice (*cont'd*)

Lose professional. Nup, put professional back in. That's important. Lose competitive and expert. Slashing and burning here, sort of. Combine of integrity and ethical? I think of integrity encapsulates ethical. Lose ethical.

That's it, I've got 11. Sue me.

So, here's my final list:

> **adventurous, curious, successful, professional, independent, of integrity, family-oriented, fit & healthy, loving, financially secure, respected.**

I sound magnificent!

EXERCISE 3: HOW DO I PRIORITISE MY VALUES?

Take your list of top values and rank them in order of what is most important to you.

In doing this, understand that there will be trade-offs. Your values reflect what you desire out of life for yourself, your partner, your children and the community in which you live. From time to time your values will come into conflict with one another. When this occurs you need to make a choice. For example, if one of your values is *success at work* (for instance, to reach the highest possible level in your career) while another is to be *family-oriented* (say, to be present at all of your children's major school milestones), at times something will need to give. There will be a trade-off because you can't have both of these things all of the time at the same time.

In prioritising your top values the concept of trade-offs can be confronting, and, frankly, upsetting. Your instinct might be to put your family as your top priority every single time, just because you think you should. Don't fall for this trap. To help list your priorities properly, think about the trade-offs you make each and every day as these are the decisions that reflect your true values. If you love your career and work hard at it, but generally sacrifice events involving your kids (such as school sports days), then reflect on what that means in terms of what drives you.

This is not a list of who you love most. In short, be honest with yourself: this is about living your life smarter.

Your top values are the measures you use consciously, or not, to assess whether you are really living the life you want to live. More importantly, for the purposes of getting back 30 plus hours a month:

- they will help you see whether you are investing your time where you really want to invest it; and
- they will make it much easier for you to discard the stuff that just does not float your boat.

What other women say

I could have looked after myself better. But I have actually loved this journey. It has been the ultimate in self-development.

Janine Allis

As a single mom I try to balance my work demands with how much time I spend with my kids and how much time is left for my own health (I love exercise, it's a daily priority). I still push myself the way I did when I had support.

Lucy Kippist

I work in a role that has a broad mandate but limited financial and people resources. So I make decisions every day based on a clear view of how I can be most effective in advancing

(continued)

What other women say (*cont'd*)

gender equality in Australia. My main priority for my personal time is my family. Friends, interests and personal health and wellbeing are also important, but they don't always get the priority I would like.

Kate Jenkins

Everything I do is very heart driven. When I lead with the heart it feels authentic. It just works. I also invest in my people – in their wellness – it needs to be people before profit.

Angie Weston

I found my own way of contributing. I ran a children's book club on the weekends once a month. I bought the books for all the kids and I would arrange for authors to come and speak. I even created a newsletter. The kids loved it!

Kelly Grigsby

Considering, defining, then ranking your core values is hard work. It takes deep thinking and self-reflection, and while it can be affirming (I am living my life pretty well and quite closely aligned to what's most important to me), at this point in The 5 SMART Steps, it has probably flushed out a few anomalies (*Why am I doing so much of this and not so much of that?*). No-one said this would be easy. In particular, trade-offs (or opportunity costs) are common, and regardless of the decisions you make as to where you spend your time, your choices will invariably bring some guilt (refer back to mistake #6).

Alice

God, this is hard. I feel like I should say family-oriented is my number one, but in all honesty I think that success at work is up there too. I mean, look at all the work values I had on my original list!

But, if I had to choose between spending five hours winning a great new client and getting that buzz of success *or* spending five hours watching a dance recital to see Olive in a five-minute dance, I choose work. Every single time. It's an absolute no-brainer. That doesn't mean I don't love Olive more than life itself; it just means that I would rather poke my eye out with a stick than watch a five-hour dance recital.

True.

Okay. Now I feel like a bad mom. The guilt is kicking in.

No, I'm not a bad mom! I'm just being honest. There is plenty I love about being a mom. Just not dance recitals. Success is important to me. God, just get over it Alice. Okay, here we go:

- Successful
- Family-oriented
- Fit & healthy
- Loving
- Of integrity
- Financially secure
- Adventurous
- Curious
- Respected
- Independent

Okay, good. Finally decided to get rid of 'professional' — it doesn't feel as strong as the other values. Down to 10. That will do. I have 10 values.

I actually feel pretty good about my list.

Reflection

Great work! Now you know:

- your personal time pain points — what keeps getting in your way. This is what we are going to focus on making sure we fix.
- how you are feeling right now about this life you are living.
- your values, in order of priority — the non-negotiables that you will always get out of bed for. This is where you should be investing most of your time.

Something to think about: your values, or the order of their priority, will change depending on where you are at in your life, so come back to them and reflect on them regularly.

Let's move on to step 2 of The 5 SMART Steps, which involves mapping your time.

Step 2
Map

Ask most people what they do all day, and they can't tell you exactly where their time goes. This isn't unusual. But how can you expect to invest your time smarter, including getting rid of your time-wasting habits, when you don't know exactly where you currently spend your time?

The best piece of business advice I ever received was from one of my mentors, Greg, and it was this: 'Data is King. Always lead with the data.' You need to collect the data on exactly where you are currently investing your time so you can start making some smarter decisions.

To ensure you get the data you need, step 2—Map—will help you undertake a personal time investment audit. This can be as extensive as you like, but as a minimum I want you to map one day. If you can map three days, all the better, because obviously all days are not the same. Without exception, people who map their time in detail across a number of days and record every single time they change task, achieve much more impactful results than those who adopt a less rigorous approach. Yes, time mapping can be tedious and irritating, but the data you get is phenomenal and it will change your life.

In short, mapping your time in detail may cause some short-term discomfort, but your long-term gains will be worth it. So, suck it up: you need to invest your time to find your lost time.

At the end of step 2—Map—you will have a clear idea of what:

- a typical day looks like for you
- a dream day would look like.

Alice

So, I have this book – *Me First*. I'm supposed to get back 30 hours of lost time a month. Yeah, right. There is no way I can find 30 extra hours a month. No way. I know for a fact that I am busier than a blue-arsed fly. I am up early and I keep going until it's late. Go, go, go. But it would be nice to have an extra 30 hours a month. Hell, that's … hang on, let me get my calculator … 360 extra hours a year! Who would have thought I would need a calculator to add that one up? Maybe I should give this a proper go. Because, in all honesty, there aren't enough hours in my day to get it all done.

Okay, so what exactly do I do all day? If I track my time in detail I guess I'll see the stuff which is a waste of my time, and then I can get rid of it. Is that the process? Plus it would be good to get an idea of what I need to do, what I don't need to do and what I can do better, quicker or smarter. I know what I need to stop doing: checking Facebook and searching for old boyfriends or the girls I disliked at school. Not a good use of my time. But rewarding, especially when they have gone to pasture and have lost their hair (the ex-boyfriends, not the girls). However, a former female nemesis going bald can bring a smile to my face too …

And yet I diverge. Distractions, clearly another time-wasting problem for me.

I am very good at multitasking. Really, I am. Few can whip up a stir fry while coming up with three reasons why Australia should be a republic for a school assignment while running the vacuum over the spilt noodles. I am 'the' champion of multitasking.

But I do get a bit bogged down on emails. I pop in and out of those damned messages every time I hear a *ping* from my device. Why do I do this? Got to stop the compulsive email thing.

I am bloody good at sitting down and focusing on managing my clients. I love it – it energises me. I get lots done when I'm in pure work mode – in flow.

What should I make for dinner tonight? Maybe spaghetti bolognese. I have everything I need. Oh damn it, no mince. I need to run down to the supermarket to grab some mince. Need milk too.

Ping … a new email!

Hello? Hello? Where did you go … ?

Every single day seems to be as full and demanding as the one before. It never, ever stops. You never, ever stop. You manage your home, your family, your career or business, your team and your down time (your what?). On top of this, from a technology perspective you are constantly switched on and constantly accessible: you often check your phone within 10 minutes of waking up and you continue to check it regularly throughout the day until you go to bed. At the time of writing this, the average person spends four hours a day on their mobile device, with half of that time being on social-media platforms. This is a number that is increasing year on year.

So, let's map your time.

EXERCISE 1: MY TYPICAL DAY

Monitoring where you currently spend your time is key to improving how you invest your time. This involves recording what you do over a given period, and noting every time you change task.

Below is a time sheet that will allow you to record how you spend one typical day in real time (for the purposes of this exercise, Alice has also only completed one day). You can print out more time sheets from the free resources page at www.timestylers.com. I am often asked if there are apps for recording time. Yes, there are hundreds. However, I find it more efficient and far more accurate to simply use pen and paper for this one.

In the 'Task' column, from the minute you get up until the minute you go to bed I want you to write down in shorthand how long each task takes you and what that task is: every call, every email, every interruption (and from whom), every time you are distracted or stop for a chat … everything. Do this in real time—there is no point trying to recreate your day at the end of the day because you will miss all the little filler tasks. Also, don't fudge the data: if you spend an hour on social media, then write it down. We'll complete columns 2 (Must/Want/Delegate/Reject) and 3 ($ spend) in step 3—Analyse.

Time	Task	Must/Want/ Delegate/ Reject	$ spend
5–6 am			
6–7 am			
7–8 am			
8–9 am			
9–10 am			
10–11 am			
11 am– 12 pm			
12–1 pm			
1–2 pm			
2–3 pm			
3–4 pm			
4–5 pm			
5–6 pm			
6–7 pm			
7–8 pm			
8–9 pm			

9–10 pm			
10–11 pm			
11 pm–12 am			
12–1 am			

Alice

Okay, here I go …

Time	Task
5–6 am	Sleep
6–7 am	Get up / dress 30 min. jog 10 min. shower, incl. wiping down walls 10 min. make brekky for myself and kids 5 min. eat brekky 5 min. stand in front of fridge and make mental shopping list
7–8 am	10 min. make kids' lunches 10 min. tidy up after brekky 10 min. find Henry's sports clothes 5 min. nag kids to brush teeth 15 min. get dressed and throw on makeup 5 min. pack my bag 5 min. yell at kids to hurry up
8–9 am	10 min. drive kids to school 30 min. drive into town, making work calls 5 min. park car and walk to office 10 min. grab takeaway coffee 5 min. 'hellos' as I walk to my office
9–10 am	10 min. check emails 10 min. on Facebook — networking? 40 min. work
10–11 am	60 min. client X

(continued)

Alice (*cont'd*)

11 am–12 pm	60 min. client Y
12–1 pm	15 min. grab some sushi 20 min. at supermarket getting essentials for dinner 15 min. eat sushi while checking Facebook 10 min. make cup of coffee and chat
1–2 pm	15 min. client Z 5 min. interruption from Bill 10 min. check emails 30 min. back to client Z
2–3 pm	5 min. fresh air 5 min. chat to John on the phone 20 min. client Z 5 min. interruption from Kaye 15 min. emails 10 min. client Z
3–4 pm	10 min. client Z 15 min. chat with Jill 10 min. coffee and chat with Al 15 min. emails 10 min. invoicing
4–5 pm	10 min. invoicing 15 min. interruption from Bill 10 min. invoicing 25 min. clear emails / tidy desk
5–6 pm	5 min. run to car 30 min. drive to school to collect kids, making work calls 5 min. drive kids to after-school activities, making work calls. Drop Olive at dance class (there is no way I am going to stay and watch!) and Henry at basketball. 20 min. dash home and clean kitchen, chuck some chemicals down the toilet and give a quick brush and flush, stand in front of fridge again thinking about what I need

6–7 pm	5 min. bring washing in and combine it with yesterday's pile of washing 20 min. start dinner 5 min. pick kids up from activities 5 min. get kids set up with homework 15 min. start folding washing, help with homework, turn on bath, put chickens away and collect eggs, feed cat, feed dog 10 min. keep an eye on dinner, tidy kitchen — working like a maniac here
7–8 pm	15 min. get kids in bath, finish dinner prep (tidying as I go), set table 20 min. get kids out of bath, yell at them to stop fighting, yell at them to get into their PJs, yell at them to put their homework away, put their homework away myself, yell at them to get their lunchboxes out of their bags, get the lunchboxes out of their bags myself, yell at them to put their folded clothes away, do that myself too 25 min. eat dinner
8–9 pm	20 min. read with kids 10 min. cuddle kids and put them to bed, try not to fall asleep myself 20 min. talk with John. Who? Oh yes, I remember you. My husband. 10 min. vacuum kitchen floor, finish the dishes, put leftovers away
9–10 pm	15 min. tidy up all the kids' crap 20 min. check Facebook 10 min. check diary for tomorrow, fall asleep on couch 5 min. get ready for bed Sleep

Huh?

Looking over your typical day can be daunting. The first thing you might think is, *Wow, I do a lot!* You might even think, *Wow, I spend a lot of my time on a whole lot of crap!*

The important thing at this stage of The 5 SMART Steps is not to judge yourself. The whole point of reading *Me First* is because you want to change. You wouldn't be reading this if you were already living the life that you wanted. You are reading *Me First* because you *want more time* (and some help in getting there).

I mean, where did you actually think your extra 30 plus hours were going to come from? It's not magic. Obviously the time you get back at the end of *Me First* has to come from reworking the time you already have. So stick with me and let's get on with it.

Now, for a change of pace I want you to consider your dream day. How would a much better day pan out for you?

EXERCISE 2: MY DREAM DAY

Exactly what would your best day ever look like? Not the dream day where you drink champagne with Brad Pitt on a private beach in Bali. This is about the dream day where your typical day gets a whole lot better, and you actually invest time where you really want to invest it.

Fill out the time sheet below and only include the things that would make your day better: from a half-hour sleep-in; how long you take to get ready; sitting down at your desk without procrastinating and working in a goal-oriented way through your most important tasks; minimal emails; no meetings; no interruptions; coming home to a clean house; washing has been done; meal is prepared; time for a soothing bath before spending time with your family, who are all calm and clean and speak nicely to one another.

My dream day—time sheet

Time	Task
5–6 am	
6–7 am	
7–8 am	
8–9 am	
9–10 am	
10–11 am	
11 am–12 pm	
12–1 pm	
1–2 pm	
2–3 pm	
3–4 pm	
4–5 pm	
5–6 pm	
6–7 pm	
7–8 pm	
8–9 pm	
9–10 pm	
10–11 pm	

Alice

Time	Task
5–6 am	Sleeping peacefully after not waking or stirring once, no-one had a nightmare, no-one had a temperature, John didn't snore. Wake feeling extraordinarily refreshed. Who is this woman?
6–7 am	30 min. jog with John (snort) and feel even better! 10 min. shower, but no need to wipe it down as it's already clean Kids are already up and they have made, eaten and put away their own brekky and loaded the dishwasher (hahaha!) 20 min. make my own brekky, eat it in peace, kids get themselves organised without whinging
7–8 am	No need to make kids' lunches as they have done it themselves! 25 min. get dressed, put on some proper makeup. Kids tell me how nice I look. John says I am one red hot sexy woman. Brad Pitt calls — oh, no, sorry forgot it's dream day not fantasy day. 35 min. ummm ... spare time, chat to John
8–9 am	Kids want to ride their bikes to school, together, on their own, without me. No tears, no drama, no fights. They even appear to like each other. 5 min. wave kids off and smile lovingly at the candid camera, as surely there must be one hiding in the bushes 15 min. drive to work because there is no traffic 5 min. park car 30 min. morning meeting in the coffee shop 5 min. cleaner calls to see if I would like him to prepare dinner tonight ... um, yes please

9 am–3 pm	Awesomely efficient @ work, working seamlessly from client file to client file with absolutely no interruptions Pop out for an hour to meet John for lunch in town. OMG it's a day date!
3–4 pm	5 min. get in car and leave work early 15 min. drive home — no traffic. Arrive home at the same time as the kids. 40 min. make afternoon tea with the kids, spend quality time with them talking about their day; they remember what they did and they answer me in full sentences; no-one wants the TV on; everyone is happy and smiling because we are a happy, smiling, non-TV-watching, blissfully beautiful family where everyone is kind, considerate and encouraging of each other; no-one checks their phone Feeling relaxed and enjoying the company of my kids The house has been cleaned to within an inch of its life and dinner is prepared. Kids promise not to mess up the house — and they don't! John arrives home early, with flowers
4–5 pm	30 min. drive kids to after-school activities and decide not to just drop-and-run; stay and watch; kids thrilled; catch up with other parents 5 min. cleaner calls and reminds me I don't need to go to the supermarket because he shopped for us today — bless him 5 min. drive home from activities 20 min. kids do their homework with John so I go for a walk with the dog. Dog delighted.

(continued)

Alice (*cont'd*)

5–6 pm	Kids have done their homework and they tidy it away! 20 min. kids feed pets and play in the backyard. Reminds me of my childhood. 40 min. John and I enjoy a G&T and chat about our day. Kids don't interrupt.
6–7 pm	60 min. eat dinner all together and share great conversation with the kids — we are just like those families you see on TV!
7–8 pm	60 min. kids clear dinner away, load dishwasher, tidy the kitchen, put chickens away, run their own bath, hang up their own towels so I can sit and chill with John, again. Hello John — aren't our kids amazing and look how blissfully happy we all are.
8–9 pm	60 min. we play a family board game. I swear to God I am not kidding.
9–10 pm	20 min. kids go to bed without any fuss 40 min. John and I watch our favourite TV show
10–11 pm	I stay up later than usual because I am not dog tired. John and I even have the strength and desire to head to the boudoir (dream day, right?)

Reflection

Great work! Now you know:

- exactly what your typical day looks like. Confronting, yes?
- exactly what your dream day looks like. And yes, it's a *dream* for the very reason that it feels completely unattainable right now. But let's go glass half full here ladies—even if you got 50 per cent towards your dream day, that's still 50 per cent better than you are living right now, right?

Something to think about: you are really clear on your typical day (let's call it your Point A) and you are really clear on where you want to be—your dream day (Point B)—so why is it that you aren't there already?

It's time to *analyse* your time maps to find hours of lost time.

Step 3

Analyse

In step 3 of The 5 SMART Steps you will categorise your time into one of four different time categories, and then you will cost your time habits. And when it comes to your costs, trust me, it won't be pretty.

Alice

I don't actually think I am that bad when it comes to managing my time. I know I have my bad days, but on the whole I am a successful woman — I get stuff done. Just look at my typical day — I couldn't jam another thing in!

Oh yeah, right, that's not actually a good thing here. That's like proving I am the best at being stupidly busy.

I guess I have always been the go-to girl: 'Give it to Alice because it will get done' is what they say. That's just how I rock, and I guess I like it. But that's no longer the right answer. In fact, that's half the problem.

I do wonder ... my dream day looks blissful. Maybe I will print it out and keep it close. Is it achievable?

Break it down, Baby

Each task you perform every day falls into one of the following four time categories:

1. *Must*—these are tasks that you, and only you, can do. For example:
    - eat
    - sleep
    - attend that important client meeting
    - one-on-one with your boss.
2. *Want*—these are tasks you love to do when you have the time. For example:
    - exercise
    - read
    - garden
    - meditate
    - family time.
3. *Delegate*—these are tasks that can be done by someone else. On the home front there are two forms of delegation: outsourcing and insourcing.

    Outsourcing is where you identify all the tasks you perform that you are prepared to pay someone else, an expert, to do because they will do the task faster, better and cheaper than you. For example:

    - cleaning
    - gardening
    - window washing.

Insourcing is where you identify all the tasks you perform for the people you live with that they can do for themselves and that you don't have to pay for. For example:

- put away your crap
- clean up your floordrobe
- hang up your towel
- put the empty toilet roll in the bin.

4 *Reject*—these are the tasks you can reject. Go figure. There are two forms of rejects: partial rejects and total rejects.

 Partial rejects are the tasks that have to be done but where you can be a whole lot smarter about how and when you do them. For example (not) going to the supermarket five times a week.

 Total rejects are the tasks that no-one needs to do, ever. For example:

 - going anywhere during peak hour
 - ironing (seriously—don't buy clothes that need to be ironed).

EXERCISE 1: MUST, WANT, DELEGATE OR REJECT?

Based on the above definitions, complete the 'Must/Want/Delegate/Reject' column of the time sheet in part 2—Map ('My typical day—time sheet', page 92), labelling each task as a must, a want, or something that you might be able to delegate or reject.

Keep the following in mind.

If for any given task you are tossing up between the task being a Must or a Want, don't spend too much time worrying about this. Just choose the category that has the stronger pull for you and move on quickly.

If there are tasks that you feel obliged to allocate to a Must or Want by virtue of pure guilt, this is a trap. Be honest. If you dread a task, then that's a pretty good indication that it's up for grabs as a Delegate or Reject.

At this stage, don't worry about how you are going to delegate or reject tasks. I just want you to be aware of what is potentially up for grabs.

Remember, the tasks you ultimately delegate or reject are the ones where you are going to find all of your lost time.

Alice

I need to eat — so that's a Must. And sleep is a Must.

Family time and eating dinner together — that's a Want.

Cleaning tasks? I'd love to Delegate those.

Olive's dance class — OMG, I hate dance. Mother's guilt. Mother's guilt. It has to be a Reject? Or maybe I can Delegate it to Mom? John?

Facebook — I love it, I love it, I love it ... but at work? And so often? There is no point pretending I'm using it strategically to grow the business because my clients aren't on there ... Reject? Hmmmm.

Somewhere along the line I turned from mother and provider to maid. I seem to spend half my life driving them around and the other half cleaning up after them. Surely they are old enough to start doing the basics for themselves? Delegate. And John — he's old enough too.

I love my job. Want? Must? Want? Must? Look, realistically it's a Must because I need to make a living, and a Want should really be something awesome like a massage? Work = Must.

Jogging. Want.

EXERCISE 2: HOW MUCH TIME I CAN POTENTIALLY RECLAIM

Add up the total time you spend on the tasks you have identified (up until this stage) as being a potential Delegate or Reject. Then multiply the time spent by 30 (days) to give yourself a reasonable estimate of how much time you could potentially reclaim each month (if you were to delegate and reject every task you have identified in these categories so far).

A	The number of hours I will save each day if I delegate everything in my Delegate list	
B	The number of hours I will save each day if I discard or better manage everything in my Reject list	
C	(A + B) × 30 days = the number of hours I can get back a month	

Remember, this is only your first time cut and nothing is set in concrete—the hours you save will change as you continue to work through The 5 SMART Steps.

Alice

Okay, let's do this.

A	The number of hours I will save each day if I delegate everything in my Delegate list	50 mins
B	The number of hours I will save each day if I discard or better manage everything in my Reject list	35 mins

(continued)

Alice (*cont'd*)

C	(A + B) × 30 days = the number of hours I can get back a month	50 + 35 = 85 mins 85 × 30 = 2550 mins 2500 / 60 = 42.5 hrs

Really? What? Wow ...

If that doesn't motivate you to take action to change your time habits, then I am pretty sure the section below on the four cost lenses will get you across the line.

What are your time habits really costing you?

You have a great career or a great business and you have come this far based on sheer talent and lots of hard work. But time is short. You have already seen from your typical day that your schedule is pretty full. There is no room for more. And it doesn't matter how talented you are—if you don't have any time left to give, how can you take yourself to the next level in your career or the next growth stage in your business?

Your current time investment habits represent a big threat to your ongoing success. How so? Because regardless of how well you currently invest your time, your habits (and your toleration of the habits of those around you) are costing you.

An effective use of your time is where the vast majority of your time is spent on your Musts and Wants. Most likely, however, what you have discovered so far is that the way you currently use your time is not always the best investment of your time.

And just what is this costing you? Probably a whole lot more than you thought.

The four cost lenses

Don't take a guess at what your time habits are costing you. Remember—Data is King, and we want the data. Understanding exactly what your habits are costing you will:

- motivate you to implement different time investment habits
- help you truly value your time (because if you don't place a value on your time, no-one else will)
- help you decide whether any given task is the best use of your time.

There are four cost lenses that you need to keep front of mind when it comes to smart time investment:

- *Financial cost*—this is the cost to you in dollar terms of each task you perform. Bottom line—your time is money.
- *Opportunity cost*—each time you choose to perform a particular task there will always be a trade-off. Your opportunity cost is the cost of what you just gave up.
- *Emotional cost*—this cost comes into play when you feel bad, or guilty, or frustrated about how you spent your time.
- *Physical cost*—if any given task makes for pain, then that is the physical cost associated with how you just spent your time.

For every task you choose to invest your time in, there will always be a financial cost (because your time is money) and there will always be an opportunity cost (because there will always be something else you could have done). Emotional cost and physical cost will often, but not always, come into play.

The key is to identify which cost lens resonates most strongly with you, as that is the lens you need to look through when it comes to choosing what tasks you are going to invest your precious time in.

EXERCISE 3: WHAT ARE MY COSTS?

The purpose of this exercise is to have you think more deeply about what your time is worth in financial (dollar) terms and in terms of the opportunity, emotional and physical costs you incur when you do not invest your time well.

Financial cost

If you or your employer currently charge your time out by the hour, I want you to use this as your hourly rate for every task you perform, even for non-remunerated and home-based tasks.

If you don't charge your time out by the hour, a quick way to calculate a sufficiently accurate hourly rate is to divide your gross income by the number of hours you work per annum (for example, if you work 50 hours a week, then you work 2600 hours per annum). You don't need to calculate this to the last cent—just round it to the nearest dollar to make life simple:

My hourly rate is $ ______________.

Using your hourly rate, complete the '$ spend' column of the time sheet in part 2—Map ('My typical day—time sheet', page 92) by noting the financial cost for each task you perform. For example, if your hourly rate is $100 and you spend 15 minutes in the shower, then note down $25 next to that task.

Next, add up the daily financial cost for the tasks you have identified as Must tasks and multiply that number by 30 to determine your average monthly financial spend for your Must tasks. Repeat this equation for your Want tasks, and then for your Delegate tasks and finally your Reject tasks. You can see an extract of how Alice went about this.

Alice

My employer charges my time out to my clients at $100 per hour, so from now on that is my hourly rate for all the tasks I perform, even the chores I do at home. It certainly puts things in a different light.

Task and time spent	Monthly financial cost based on an hourly rate of $100
1 hour a day on social media	30 days × 1 hour × $100 = $3000
3 hours a workday on administrative tasks	20 days x 3 hours x $100 = $6000
4 hours a week cleaning my house	4 weeks x 4 hours x $100 = $1600

You get the idea—your time is money. Even if you were to find and harness half an hour a day @ $100 an hour, that's $18 250 of your time a year. Feeling motivated?

The above methodology will give you a good approximation of what your time is worth in dollar terms and, assuming you repeat most tasks day in and day out, it is likely that you have been spending many hours (and many dollars) investing your time in tasks that no-one in their right mind would pay you for at your hourly rate.

If the financial cost layer is your hot spot, this is the question I want you to constantly ask yourself for each task you perform: *Is this really the best use of my time?*

What other women say

As a lawyer, you balance financial cost with opportunity cost. These two cost lenses resonate most with me, but can sometimes be in conflict. I have spent years mastering the delivery of value through billable time. Because of this, the dollar value of my time has always been clear. But, you can't put a dollar value on lost opportunity, particularly when it comes to family. I try to focus on my values so that an assessment of both financial cost and opportunity cost is embedded in where I choose to invest my time.

Jane Hall

Opportunity cost

Unfortunately, your financial costs are not the worst of it. Opportunity cost is associated with anything of value (financial or otherwise, such as a lost benefit or a lost pleasure) that you give up to acquire or achieve something else. Put simply—your trade-offs.

Extending Alice's examples under financial costs above, in addition to the financial cost associated with the tasks you choose to invest in, there will always be an opportunity cost.

Alice

I'm sure I'm missing out on all sorts of opportunities for Me Time. Let's have a look ...

Task and time spent	Sample opportunity costs
1 hour a day on social media	1 hour at the gym; meditating; spending time with my family; landing a new client
3 hours per workday on administrative tasks	3 hours on myriad strategic, partnership and client opportunities

4 hours cleaning my house	4 hours spent on myself; a long lunch with friends; catching up with family; rest and relaxation; sleep

Eight hours of lost time! I knew it — this just isn't right!

If the opportunity cost lens is the cost that resonates most strongly with you, then when it comes to choosing where to invest your time, I want you to ask yourself this question: *What is the trade-off here? What am I missing out on?*

If the trade-off isn't worth it and the opportunity cost is too great, make a better choice.

For me, financial cost and opportunity cost generally resonate the most.

What other women say

There is always a sacrifice to make.

Caroline Jean-Baptiste

Opportunity cost is my main consideration. In my personal life I consider whether I would rather spend the time at home with my family, or whether the activity would be fun to do with my family. My time on the Carlton Football Club board brought much pleasure to my family, as well as being a great professional experience. Go Blues!

Kate Jenkins

I realised a while ago that every decision I make means I'm trading precious chunks of my life for a social construct, mostly money or good manners. So I try and always make choices that give me the most joy or are worthwhile, not just those that tick boxes.

Kate Halfpenny

Emotional cost

The emotional cost of how you choose to invest your time is a huge issue for women juggling career and family. There is a constant tension between our drive to succeed at work and our desire to be present with our children. There will be times when you are needed at work but equally needed at home. So, what do you do? You need to choose, and your choice will be informed by both rational decision making and by emotional decision making. And sometimes you will make the wrong choice. And when you do? Well, you know what happens—you are racked with guilt, you beat yourself up, you question your values and priorities, and you self-talk up a virtual tornado of criticism and self-loathing.

Emotional cost is where you feel you invested your time well, or not—these costs generally include feelings of stress, guilt and self-judgement about whether you made the right choice.

If emotional cost is your hot spot, the question I want you to constantly ask yourself for each task you perform is this: *How am I going to feel about this later?*

Alice

Don't even get me started on emotional cost.

What other women say

Emotional cost: is the money worth it for not seeing my daughters? Nine times out of ten it's not, and so I won't do it.

Alexandra Depledge

This is such a great exercise. It really makes you reflect on where and how you spend your time — what drives your decisions. For me, emotional cost gazumps even opportunity cost, which I find interesting. Maybe it's the good Catholic girl in me?

Carmel Mulhern

I don't want to go to bed with a 'racy' mind. Good sleep is one of the things I value. I've done enough sleepless nights in the past.

Julie McDonald

Physical cost

The final cost layer is physical cost. This one isn't rocket science. If the task you have chosen to invest your time in makes for pain, then this is a physical cost on top of your other costs.

By way of example, if you spend 12 hours a day working and fail to exercise, there will be a physical cost associated with this lifestyle pattern.

If physical cost is your hot spot, the question I want you to constantly ask yourself for each task you perform is this: *Is this going to make for pain and slow me down?*

Alice

I think it is pretty clear that when you vacuum with one arm while leaning your weight on the nearest surface with the other arm so you can support the pain in your lower back, that's probably a good indication that vacuuming is exacting a physical cost. I can't afford for my back to go again. Last time I was in bed unable to move for four days and I had to crawl to and from the toilet. When I was finally upright I looked like the Leaning Tower of Pisa. The physio told me that to get better I needed to 'get in touch with my pelvic floor': 'Dear Pelvic Floor, It has been some time since we were last in touch. I recall vaguely having some contact with you before Henry was born, but gee, that would be a good 11 years ago! So, how the hell have you been?'

Yeah, right. Ciao, ciao Pelvic Floor … it was nice knowing you.

EXERCISE 4: STRESS TEST MY TASK CATEGORIES

The four cost lenses have given you a different perspective of how and where you want to invest your time—and the fact that some of your habits are costing you way too much!

For each task on your time sheet that you initially identified as a Must or a Want, but which you now know the cost of is too high (either in a financial, opportunity, emotional and/or physical sense), consider whether these tasks can be delegated or rejected, and mark up your changes to your time sheet.

Again, at this point in time, don't worry about how you are going to achieve the switch from doing the task to not doing the task—we will get to that later.

Alice

Based on the costs to me of investing my time in this way, there are actually *a lot more* tasks here that I can delegate or reject. Interesting. I need to sort this stuff out. Soon.

- *Making the kids' lunches* — I actually enjoy this (strange, I know) and it also means I know that they are getting a healthy, nutritional lunch. If I left it up to them to make their own lunch, God knows what they would choose to eat. But, I do plan to educate them on this better. I will get them to make their lunches with me. That way they can learn what is good to eat and I can also transition them to making their own lunch.
- *Driving the kids to school* — maybe I'll just drive them on rainy days and the rest of the time they can ride their bikes. They are old enough and it will give them a greater sense of independence, plus it will save me so much time.

- *Setting the kids up for homework* – I can do this a bit smarter. Like making the lunches, I will work alongside the kids so they can learn how to set themselves up properly, and then I will help them with anything they don't understand.
- *School pick-up* – if I delegate school pick-up, then I won't have to rush home in such a frenzy. Plus, whoever I delegate this to can start the meal prep for me. Hey, this is a smart idea! Imagine how much time I will save on the peak hour commute!
- *Clearing the table* – it also makes sense to delegate clearing of the table to the kids. If we split this up, then both John and I can put the kids to bed together. There is so much more the kids can do.

Damn it, I still feel guilty about not watching Olive at dance class. She keeps asking me to stay and watch 'like the other moms'. And I know some moms can think of nothing more joyous than watching their child hop around in a pink tutu, but not me. But, if I don't do it I'll continue to be racked with guilt. I hate mother's guilt! I know family-oriented is my second priority, but too bad. I just can't do dance. The 'emotional cost' of watching her dance is actually higher than the emotional cost of not watching her dance. I will do something else with her.

EXERCISE 5: HOW DO I FEEL?

Analysing where you currently invest your time, and what that is costing you, is challenging. This is completely understandable: you are breaking down your time and analysing it to within an inch of its life. It's bound to be confronting!

Write down a few thoughts about how you feel right now.

Alice

How do I feel?

My God. I can't believe this. I knew that I was doing the lion's share of chores around the house, and that it probably wasn't the best use of my time, but costing it out financially finally proves to me that I have been living like a lunatic. And I thought I was using my time quite well. I was deluded.

I haven't even started on my weekends yet.

My hourly rate is $100. It took me four hours to clean the house on Sunday — damn, that clean just cost me $400! Plus if I factor in that I was cleaning on my day off, eating into family time, and on a Sunday (penalty rates, surely?), the opportunity cost is ridiculous. I could have an expert clean my house for around $25 an hour — and because they are an expert they will clean in three hours not four, which will cost $75 and buy me back four hours of my own time ... I want to weep.

And then I think about what I could have been doing with those four hours: a family adventure (living my values, right!?), reading a book and relaxing, going for a bike ride with the kids.

Speaking of kids, tidying up after the kids for three hours a week is costing me $300! Every week! And going to the supermarket four or five times a week is costing me a fortune.

John is going to have a heart attack when I tell him that his efforts at mowing the lawn (pretty badly if the truth be known) cost us $200. Ha!

Crud. It's not funny.

EXERCISE 6: MY TOTAL SAVINGS

Before we finish step 3—Analyse—and now that you have updated your time sheets and found even more tasks you can delegate or reject, let's update the table from exercise 2 earlier to work out how many lost hours you have identified as hours you can potentially reclaim.

This is the best bit!

A	The number of hours I will save each day if I delegate everything in my Delegate list	
B	The number of hours I will save each day if I discard or better manage everything in my Rejects list	
C	(A + B) x 30 days = the number of hours I can get back a month	

Reflection

Great work! Now you know:

- your Musts, Wants, Delegates and Rejects
- the four costs associated with how you invest your time
- exactly what you can Delegate or Reject because doing these tasks no longer makes sense.

Here are some things to consider:

- Consciously think about the tasks you are choosing to invest your time in and keep asking yourself: *Is this really the best use of my time?* If it's not, make a better choice.
- Not all time is created equal. Some tasks, such as choosing to watch your kids play sport or going on a date with your partner instead of spending an additional two hours at work may not be the best use of your time financially; however, you will gain enormous happiness and satisfaction from your decision. Other activities, such as sitting at your desk without a break, might result in a clean inbox for the day, but are not necessarily the best use of your time physically.

It's time to *reframe*.

Step 4

Reframe

The potential number of hours you can reclaim as identified at the end of step 3—Analyse—may seem to you to be a little, well, unreal. However, don't forget that those savings reflect what is up for grabs if you choose to Delegate and Reject every single task you have identified. You may not choose to do so. All we are aiming for at this point in time is to reclaim one lost hour a day (30 hours a month).

You need to trust the process.

What other women say

When I was appointed CEO, I worked with Kate and she helped me reframe my time – it was a game changer for me. In part I think it was just external validation from someone else that it's okay to be a mom and an executive and that I needed to focus my time where it was most needed at any given time, and if that was with my daughter, then that was okay.

Kelly Grigsby

Step 4—Reframe—is all about the *how*: how do you take the data you have collected so far and turn it into reality? Step 4 will show you how to move from a position of doing absolutely everything for the little blood suckers you live with, to not doing everything for them — there are plenty of tasks you can delegate. Step 4 will also show you how to discard your rejects. You will soon see why Delegate and Reject are my favourite time categories.

Historian Will Durant summed up Aristotle's many musings on habits thus: 'We are what we repeatedly do. Excellence, then, is not an act, but a habit'. And who are we to argue with Aristotle? We are creatures of habit: we wake and fall into the flow of our day, each day, every day, much in the same way as the day before and the one before that.

As such, from a time investment perspective, the key is to understand which of your habits are poor; how you can tweak those habits to produce an excellent outcome; and how to repeat this new level of excellence again and again until a better habit is formed. This will take work. However, if you do the work, you will get back hours of time to live a better life — a life you love. Now that has got to be worth it, yes?

With a clear idea of your Musts, Wants, Delegates and Rejects, along with the four cost lenses (financial, opportunity, emotional and physical), it's now time to reframe.

Let's quickly cover the Musts and then I want you to focus 100 per cent on your Delegates and Rejects. This is where the big wins are.

Musts

Your Musts are the essential things you need to do. The vast majority of your time will be spent on your Musts — for example, unless you are an heiress you will need to earn money, which means you will need to work. Working for a living is a Must for most of us.

Having said that, you also want to be in a position where the vast majority of your Musts are tasks you actually love, or at least enjoy doing. If not, then some serious reflection is needed to consider whether you are in the right job, or the right relationships, or the right frame of mind. Working through The 5 SMART Steps may be a key realisation for you that you actually don't enjoy some of your Musts. And if that is the case, then you have some more changes to make.

For those Musts that you don't enjoy but which are temporary (such as watching dance recitals) you either need to suck it up (this time will pass) or you need to Delegate or Reject it.

For those Musts that you don't enjoy doing all the time but are happy to do some of the time, (such as vacuuming) consider delegating the task and then jumping in when needed to keep things under control.

For those Musts that you don't enjoy at all and which take up much of your time (such as back-to-back meetings) invest the time to decide which meetings you absolutely do need to attend, which you never need to attend, which someone else can attend for you and which can be dealt with differently (such as by email).

The 5 SMART Steps is an iterative process and you will continue, forever, to refine your Musts, Delegates, Rejects and Wants.

Delegating

The reason you delegate the tasks you don't want to do, don't have the key skills to do well or don't have time to do, is to give yourself time for the things you do want to do. Go figure.

Earlier this year I ran a productivity workshop for a high-performing team and one female participant said she was going to delegate 'date night'. Everyone laughed uproariously, but the implications from her comment were this: *every single task* on the home front can be delegated. You just have to decide what you no longer want to do, and work from there.

When considering what to Delegate, keep in mind the four cost lenses discussed in step 3—Analyse—because you now know that it often makes sense to have someone else undertake some (or many) of the home-based tasks for you.

On the home front there are two forms of delegation; outsourcing and insourcing.

Outsourcing is where you identify all the tasks you perform that you are prepared to pay someone else—an expert—to do because they will do the task faster, better and cheaper than you.

Insourcing is where you identify all the tasks you perform for the people you live with that they can do for themselves and you don't have to pay for. Happily, the list of what your family can do for themselves is endless.

OUTSOURCING

Outsourcing is a simple, effective and efficient way to gain back significant hours of lost time. And there is so much that can be outsourced—for example:

1. general cleaning
2. carpet cleaning
3. window cleaning
4. cleaning out the gutters
5. housekeeping (cleaning plus tidying)
6. meal planning
7. meal preparation
8. food shopping, unpacking and putting away
9. shopping for and wrapping gifts

10 clothes washing, folding and putting away
11 ironing
12 de-cluttering your cupboards
13 de-cluttering your garage
14 arranging your hard-rubbish collection
15 sorting your unused toys and clothes and dropping them off to a charity
16 a big spring-clean
17 mowing the lawn
18 weeding the garden
19 pruning plants, planting and maintaining your garden
20 removing garden waste and taking it to landfill
21 babysitting
22 nannying
23 parent helper (a combination of nanny and someone happy to do some light cleaning and other household chores)
24 before and after school care
25 dog walking
26 pet grooming/washing
27 pet sitting
28 taking your pet to their annual check-up at the vet
29 house sitting
30 caring/companion for an elderly dependent
31 home manager/personal assistant

32 someone to wait at home for the plumber/electrician/ delivery person

33 someone to assemble your new flat-packed furniture

34 someone to program your TV

35 someone to fix your home IT issues

36 home maintenance

37 packing up and managing your house move

38 tutoring

39 someone to run your errands/collect your dry cleaning

40 someone to pay the bills

41 someone to open your mail when you are out of town

42 someone to put out and bring in the bins when you are away

43 an expert to style your living areas

44 someone to sort through your 1000 photos and put them in online albums

45 an expert to book your next holiday

46 someone to clean up your inbox and sort out your folders

47 someone to systemise your home office

48 someone to source and order the basics online: kids undies, socks, school supplies

49 an expert to clean and maintain your pool

50 an expert to clean and maintain your car.

Oh I love to outsource! The list is practically endless!

EXERCISE 1: IT'S TIME TO OUTSOURCE

The free resources page on my website (www.timestylers.com/resources) has the above list of 50 jobs you can outsource at home, along with an outsourcing template.

Print out the template and identify everything you would like to outsource at home and then choose one task to outsource immediately.

For me, engaging a cleaner is the most obvious task you can outsource immediately. When I speak to audiences of professionals about smart time investment, I used to ask for a show of hands for who has a cleaner. And it surprised me how few hands were raised! So I flipped the question around and I now ask for a show of hands for who doesn't have a cleaner. I estimate that 60 per cent of hands go up!

This continues to genuinely shock me. You are a professional. You earn good or often very, very good money, and yet you continue to clean your house yourself with the very limited hours you have left in your day. Why? Not because you love it, but because you feel you should. Get over it. Seriously.

What other women say

If my hourly earnings are $100 and someone else can do that job for $50 or $70 or $80 or even $90, I outsource.

Alexandra Depledge

If someone has more expertise than me — at work or at home — I delegate to them. I have no ego around this at all. I just want a good job done by the best person for the job. At home, outsourcing buys me back time with my family.

Carmel Mulhern

At home I outsource based on opportunity cost. At work, I delegate with a different mindset: financial cost. I know my

(continued)

What other women say (*cont'd*)

hourly rate and I ask myself, *Would I pay someone else my hourly rate to do the same task?* If the answer is *no*, then I know it is not a good use of my time.

Julie McDonald

I don't do a lot of things like cooking or cleaning: they can be done by other professionals. You have to take certain things off your plate so that you can manage.

Anu Acharya

When I first started my business I spent $140 to have my children in care one day a week. It was a lot of money for us at that time, but I knew that I was investing in the future success of my business. And this is something I share with my team.

Angie Weston

I have my groceries delivered, which has been a life-changer. I don't like to shop, so I subscribe to a 'stylist' who sends me a box of clothing items once per month. This type of support helps me focus my time on things that I enjoy, or can learn from, or that make me feel creative and inspired, or involve spending time with people I love.

Amy Henry

I outsource everything! Everything I don't want to do and everything that I'm not good at. You have to focus on what really matters, and for me that's time with my daughter.

Kelly Grigsby

I am an Indian woman who grew up in Africa, so I was used to having help around the house, but I just didn't equate that into a payment. And I didn't want to spend my money! But after I fell very ill and ended up in hospital, I now outsource everything and I stay out of the way!

Geeta Sidhu-Robb

I have a big focus on time investment since working with Kate Christie. At work, I always ask myself, *Is this really worth my time or could someone else do it so I can focus on where I can make the biggest impact for my business or for my stakeholders?* I apply a similar logic at home. If someone else can do it cheaper than me, I outsource it.

Snezana Jankulovski

Many home service providers are experts at more than one task. In addition, many will be looking for as much work as possible. So, it makes sense to batch the tasks you want to outsource and find someone who will do them all. The benefits of this approach include that you: only have to find, interview, trial and engage one person instead of two or more; only have to introduce one new person to the family; only have to show one person the way you want things done; only have to pay one person; will save money by having one super-efficient person who does the lot; and you will be offering more work to one person = win:win.

Alice

It's time to outsource

I was loving this, but now that it's actually time to convert the data and make it real I am starting to feel guilty again. Maybe I should just do this stuff myself?

No way! I'm now clever and SMART. It's time to prove my smarts. I know this is the right thing to do because:

- I am tired, angry and nasty, and I just can't go on like this. I want to be a happy, engaged and energetic mom
- the cost of doing this stuff myself does not make sense — I have done the maths. I can get someone else to do these tasks for a lot less money than it will cost me at my own hourly rate
- I can use the time I save to spend time with my family, spend time on my own or spend time on my other Wants
- I am not an expert at these tasks. Most weeks I barely get to clean the toilets. The person I get to do these

(continued)

Alice (*cont'd*)

> tasks will be an expert. I will end up with a better result in a faster time than it would have taken me. Plus, the kids won't catch a disease from the toilet.

I am not going to let anyone judge me for the decisions I make to outsource. I certainly wasn't worried about being judged for not cleaning the toilets, so let's get a bit of perspective.

Okay. Feeling better again. I might write that list out in case I get chastised by John's mom.

After costing my time it definitely makes financial sense to get a cleaner for three hours a week. It also makes a lot of sense in terms of not hurting my back again. I thought John would vote this one down, but when he saw the opportunity cost analysis – plus when we thought about the costs of hiring in additional help if I did my back and was not able to do anything at all, plus the medical costs – he was sold (but he only wants the cleaner once a fortnight at this stage – I will need to work on him).

We have agreed that we really are in desperate need to reconnect and to spend some time together without the kids. We are going to have a weekly date night. Need to arrange a babysitter. Kids feeling affronted that we want to go out together, without them. Too bad. Can't wait!

INSOURCING

The best way to insource is to make each person in your home responsible for their own stuff: they are capable of tidying away their own belongings, hanging up their own towels, making their own beds, putting away their own clothes and so on.

And for those of you without kids, but thinking of having kids, here's a tip: have as many as you can because there are plenty of jobs they can do! Family is a team sport.

What other women say

Effective communication is as important to the smooth running of a family as it is to the smooth running of a business, so we have family huddle every weekend where we sit down together and go through our diaries for the following week so we all know who has appointments, trips or special events, and everybody knows where they need to be. If any decisions have to be made then the huddle is the place to discuss and decide.

Sarah Wood

Break insourcing into two types of tasks.

A The individual 'it's your crap, deal with it' tasks:

1. Clean up your floordrobe.
2. Hang up your towel (no, not like that … spread it out so that it dries).
3. Put your dirty clothes in the laundry basket, not on your floor, the bathroom floor, the living room floor, the kitchen floor, my bedroom floor, the floor of the car.
4. Put your clean clothes in your wardrobe.
5. When I said to clean up your floordrobe (see #1), that does not mean picking up all of the clothes on your floor and putting them in the laundry. Half that stuff is clean. Put the clean clothes in your wardrobe!
6. Make your bed. Yes, it's okay if the doona is just lumped on the bed as long as it is not on the floor.
7. Put your rubbish in the bin, not on your floor.
8. Flush the toilet.

9 Change the toilet roll.

10 Put the empty toilet roll in the bin which is right next to the toilet for absolute convenience.

11 That bin is also really handy for the empty toothpaste, the empty hair products, the balls of tissues and crusty bandaids. Don't you just love a bin!

12 Put away your computer, iPod, iPhone, cords, earphones.

13 Put away your books, toys, cars, blocks, Lego, dolls, dress-ups.

14 Put away your hair ties, hair brush, hair products, hair dryer, hair straightener.

15 Put away your kinder bag, library bag, school bag, school books, pencil case, school shoes.

16 Put away your sports clothes, cricket gear, lacrosse gear, football gear, soccer gear, swimming bag, dance gear, running gear, bike, bike helmet, surfboard, skateboard, scooter, pogo stick.

17 Put your dirty, wet, muddy, smelly sports clothes in the laundry (see #3).

18 Put away your paints, paint brush, paintings, pencils, colouring books.

19 Put away your lipstick, foundation, blush, mascara, brushes, mirrors, eye liners, eyebrow pencils, eyelash curlers, sponges, creams, sprays.

20 Put away your half-eaten food, dirty plates, dirty cups, forks, knives, spoons, straws, chocolate wrappers, lolly wrappers, ice-cream wrappers, chip packets, drink bottles.

21 Unpack your school bag, throw away the rubbish, throw away the old fruit at the bottom of the bag, wash your

lunchbox, take out the school notes and give them to me, wipe out your bag because it smells.

22 Make your school lunch: there's heaps of great food in the fridge, help yourself, it's not hard.

23 Make your snack: it's in the same place as the rest of the food.

24 Change your linen: honey you are 10. I think your arms are long enough to put a doona cover on the doona.

25 Get your own towel: look, here is a cupboard full of them.

26 Don't leave your rubbish in the car.

B The 'family is a team sport, buddy, suck it up' tasks:

1 Take the bins out.

2 Bring the bins in.

3 Wash the dishes.

4 Set the table.

5 Clear the table.

6 Mom … what's for dinner? I don't know honey, what are you cooking tonight?

7 Help cook dinner.

8 Feed the pets.

9 Clean up after the pets.

10 Walk the pets.

11 Vacuum the floors.

12 See this wet thing? It's called a mop. Please mop the kitchen.

13 Mow the lawn.

14 Sweep the leaves.

15 Weed the garden.

16 Do a load of washing—that's okay, I'll show you how to use the washing machine. It's easy.

17 Put the washing out.

18 Bring the washing in.

19 Fold the washing.

20 Put the washing away.

21 Clean your shower.

22 Clean your basin.

23 Clean your toilet.

24 The shopping list is on the fridge. If you are the last one to use something then (i) put it in the bin and (ii) add it to the shopping list.

25 Pack the dishwasher.

26 Unpack the dishwasher.

27 Wash the outside of the car.

28 Clean and vacuum the inside of the car.

Your kids are capable of helping around the house. This is all about creating independent and resourceful human beings as opposed to dependent and helpless ones. After all, my sons are going to grow up to marry your daughters, so let's do them all a favour.

What other women say

Since I met Kate I use the expression 'Family is a team sport' all of the time! I had not used that phrase before. We always had a strong emphasis in our family on how we make our money, how we make a living, where a dollar comes from and how our kids are involved in that. It has been part of their upbringing — our farming business is all around them and they are all involved in it. Plus we have a rule: the first person to stop cleaning up has to finish it.

Julie McDonald

Absolutely I insource! Someone very wise (a.k.a. Kate) taught me that my kids could do so much more at home. From vacuuming and mopping, to folding and putting away clothes, ironing, making their lunches and tidying up around the house. I reward them for it (usually pocket money) so they never complain about it. Everyone in our household contributes and that means we can spend more time enjoying our weekends together.

Snezana Jankulovski

We have a great roster at home. Mind you, it's not strictly adhered to. The kids don't automatically just do their chores — not unless they are trying to butter me up for something, and suddenly they become really helpful!

Carmel Mulhern

Beware these insourcing traps

Now that you are clever and smart it's time to *be strong*.

Right about now the thought of the fights you will have in getting your kids, and maybe even your partner, to actually manage their own crap might get that little voice in your mind chattering away. Let's knock that on the head right now.

Trap 1: The 'Oh MY GODDDD, my kids/partner have left their wet towels on the floor again! How many times do I have to ask them to hang their towels up? Honestly, I am not their [insert swear word of choice] maid!' trap.

And then what do you do? You pick up the wet towels from the floor and you re-hang them. You know you do this.

Is it any wonder that your family don't pick their towels up for themselves? If you were living in a hotel where the towels you left on the bathroom floor were (miraculously it seems) collected, washed, refreshed and re-hung every single day, you would probably leave your towel on the floor too.

I am not blaming you. I am just telling you that you are a major part of the problem.

Solution: You are breaking two habits here: (i) the habit of your family who are used to leaving their crap lying around because they know you will pick it up and put it away, and (ii) your habit of picking it up and putting it away.

When there are no clean clothes to wear and they need a map to navigate the journey through their floordrobes from their bedroom door to their bed, they will get the message.

Stay strong.

Trap 2: The 'I just can't be bothered nagging my kids/partner every single day to get them to help me. I am sick of the sound of my own voice. It's just easier if I do it myself' trap.

It's true. You are sick of the sound of your own voice. And yes, it would be easier to do it yourself. But both of these small facts don't change the bigger fact that if you want to reclaim hours of lost time, you need to stop doing the basics for your family.

Solution: Your children (and partner) are entirely capable of doing this stuff for themselves. Keep in mind: you are not doing your family any favours by doing these basic, yet fundamental, tasks for them. It's never too early for your kids, and it's never too late for your partner, to learn some self-sufficiency. So if you can't let go of being their maid for your own benefit, then tell yourself that you are doing this for them. Again, your family will eventually get the message. And when they do, make sure you tell them how awesome they are (even if it did take them 9 and 45 years respectively before they learned to hang up their own towel for the first time …).

Trap 3: The 'It's not that hard for me to do the small stuff. Really. It only takes me five minutes' trap.

No, it does not. It's time for a reality check—the small stuff that you think only takes five minutes actually eats up hours and hours of your life. If you don't believe me, I urge you to conduct your own experiment on the small stuff you do.

Solution: Get the data. Keep a record for a couple of days and jot down all the crazy, time-sucking, small-stuff tasks you do that you could insource, record how long you spend on each of these tasks and then add it up. You will be horrified.

For example:

- if you spend five minutes each and every day sorting the dirty washing, that's 30 hours of your time a year
- if you spend 12 minutes each and every day tidying up all of the crap your kids leave around the house, that's 73 hours of your time a year.

You can do the maths.

Alice

Insourcing

For the purposes of my own scientific research I timed the small stuff and clearly it ain't so small after all. The small stuff certainly does not take 'five minutes'. Here are the results of my own research, rounded to the nearest hour* (*note, not performed under internationally recognised scientific conditions such as having a control group and other such

(continued)

Alice (*cont'd*)

technical requirements that I don't actually recall from high school science class. Rather, just performed by me in my own home with my watch. Plus I have assumed a 12 hour workday, not a 24 hour day because as crazy as I am, I'm not tidying up for anyone in the middle of the night.).

The small stuff I do around the house that I thought took five minutes and how long it *really* takes:

- Find the dirty washing on the floor, under the bed, on the couch, in the bathroom, in the sports bag, in the car, and put it in the wash:

  6 mins/day × 365 days/year = 3 days of my life a year
- Tidying away the devices, homework, books, shoes, basketballs, work and other kid/husband paraphernalia left out from the night before:

  12 mins/day × 365 days/year = 6 days of my life a year
- Clearing the table, putting the salt and pepper away, scraping the plates, rinsing the plates, stacking the dishwasher and wiping the table:

  7 mins/day × 365 days/year = 3.5 days of my life a year
- Folding and putting away the kids'/husband's clean clothes, clean linen and towels:

  6 mins/day × 365 days/year = 3 days of my life a year
- **Total: 15.5 days of my life a year!**

Holy Crud. John! *John!* Come here and check this out!

Trap 4: The 'Oh, my kids are too young to do chores' trap.

No they are not.

Without question, the younger you start your kids on insourcing, the better—because when they are little they are enthusiastic, compliant, everything is a game and they don't back chat. Trust me, if you leave insourcing until your kids are teenagers you will be fighting a much harder battle.

Regardless of your kids' age, as long as they can walk there are little tasks you can get them to do around the house. And if your two-year-old son can tidy away his shoes then I'm pretty confident that your 35-year-old partner is capable of the same. The older your kids get, the more complex tasks they can do.

Solution: It's important to remember you are playing a long game here. You are not after perfection when you hand your seven year old the vacuum. There is every chance you will have to re-do the job later (when they are not looking). But that's okay—this isn't about getting an amazing job done. You simply want to instil in your kids the habit of helping out at home when they are asked. That way, when your son or daughter is 15 they will vacuum like a pro, and without (too much of) an argument.

I trust you are ready to insource?

EXERCISE 2: IT'S TIME TO INSOURCE – LET'S GET MANIPULATIVE

Many of you will have terrific, helpful, wonderful partners who see the mess, clean the mess and make the kids help. Good for you—you won't need to manipulate them at all. Just have a good, healthy, open chat about who does what around the house and get on with your life.

However, I can't tell you how many times I have been asked the following question: *The kids are one thing, but how do I actually get my husband to help around the house!? He is worse than the kids …*

So, for those very many of you who have a partner who is essentially the oldest of your children, this strategy is for you.

Family is a team sport

Buy a white board.

Pre-position your partner that 'the kids' need to do more around the house, that your plan is to have a family meeting where you both discuss the fact that 'family is a team sport', and that you need to divide up the tasks around the house. You make this all about the kids. Identify the tasks you will nominate yourself for and then ask your partner to do the same.

At the family meeting you say something along the lines of, 'We are not the only ones who need to do things around the house. Family is a team sport. So from now on we are going to divide up the chores and everyone is going to help …'

At this stage you give the kids the white board and let them do the writing. Even if they are too little to write, let them hold the marker. This gives them a sense of ownership. It also feels like a game.

Then you say something along the lines of, 'I'm going to drive you to school, make dinner three times a week and walk the dogs. Honey—what are you going to do …?' Throw to your partner, who also thinks this is a game.

Your partner will blindly stumble in at this point and commit to actually doing jobs around the house: 'I'm going to make dinner twice a week, do two loads of washing a week and put all the clean clothes in your rooms for you to put away.'

Your kids need to write all of this down.

Next, ask your kids what they are going to do. This is critical. You do not want to tell them what they have to do. You want them to own this. Prompt them to suggest as much as possible. Get them to write every task down against their names. At this point they still think this is a game.

Get everyone to sign the bottom of the white board, which reads: 'This is a family contract.' Find a permanent spot in the kitchen for the white board because you are going to be referring to it every single day.

Alice

This is such a simple way to manipulate the kids (and John) that it seems cruel. But not that cruel.

I am *loving* this! There are so many jobs I can insource to my darling little loved ones that I wish I had more kids just so I had more people to insource to!

I have decided not to offer any financial incentive for these chores (apart from washing the cars). The fact is, my kids are not paying to stay at this hotel in which they reside, nor are they paying for the petrol for Mom's taxi, or the school/dentist/never-ending after-school activity fees, cash for footy cards, cash for movies, cash for hot chips after footy, cash for the sake of asking for cash. And so I am happy to let them work off some of their debt. Ha!

Besides which, *family is a team sport*. It's all about chipping in. It's all about having a good work ethic. Life wasn't meant to be easy. You weren't born with a silver spoon in your mouth. (I have hundreds of these pointless little expressions that I am happy to throw out at will as required. However, sometimes it's quite alarming when I open my mouth and my mother comes out.)

This isn't over. I am going to keep adding and adding and adding to my new insourcing list.

From now on, when you see your family's stuff lying around just begging you to pick it up, clear it away, tidy it or make it magically disappear, take a deep breath, back out of the room and quietly shut the door.

Remind your family of what they agreed to do—who cares if you are the parent who constantly reminds everyone of their chores? It's better than being the parent who constantly does all of the chores. The main thing is to be consistent. Remember the traps and avoid them.

Game over.

What other women say

My kids are pretty self-sufficient and I think that's because when you have two working parents, children learn by necessity to be self-sufficient. They learn to be responsible for everyday things such as getting homework done and timetabling playdates with friends.

Sarah Wood

In our house, we have systems that allow the kids to do things for themselves with ease — for example, we have containers in the fridge with numbers on them so they can pack the right balance of items for their lunch.

Amy Henry

We are raising boys who will know how to take care of themselves, cook, clean, wash, maintain etc. I recently had a flat tyre and rather than change it myself, I taught my nine year old how to do it. Laundry is brought down each morning in the 'get ready for school' process. Once you're 10 years or older, you make your own lunch. A great partnership and team is what makes our house work well.

Caroline Jean-Baptiste

I live in a joint family home. It might sound a little bizarre to a lot of people: we have four generations staying in the same house. It is really lovely because the children can grow up with their grandparents and great grandparents, and cousins and aunties. There is always someone at home, so, for instance, if I am travelling I don't have to worry and I can do my own things as well. My second tip is to have a good husband; we share responsibilities.

Anu Acharya

A FINAL WORD ON DELEGATING: DO IT THE SMART WAY

The number-one reason leaders give for not delegating at work is that they feel it is a time-consuming process that more often than not does not render the result they want, which means rework for them. And so they think, *It is easier if I just do it myself.*

You already know that this is not the right answer because if you continue to do everything for yourself you will quickly run out of time.

It's all about delegating the SMART way.

When you delegate, the aim is for the service provider (professional or child/partner) to deliver the same as or a better result than if you undertook the task yourself. The key to getting the best result the first time is to give clear and specific instructions upfront.

The standard (wrong way) to delegate is by using the SAT method:

Select:	Select the person for the task.
Activity:	Explain the details of the task.
Timeframe:	Set a deadline for delivery.

The SAT method does not provide the service provider with anywhere near enough information, and it is very likely they will produce a result that you are not entirely happy with.

The better way to delegate is by using the SMART method:

Select:	Select the person for the task.
Motivate:	Explain why the task is important (to you, for the family, for them).
Activity:	Explain the details of the task.
Result:	Explain what a good result will look like (tell them the outcome you want).
Timeframe:	Set a deadline for delivery.

SMART delegation will literally only take you a few minutes more than SAT delegation but this time investment is worth it—it will increase the prospect of the service provider producing a great result the first time, minimising the amount of time on rework and cost (financial, emotional, opportunity and physical).

Rejecting

I love the Rejects time category almost as much as the Delegates. This is where you will pick up enormous amounts of time to add to your 30 plus hours of lost time a month.

Rejects fall into two camps:

- *total rejects:* the tasks that no-one needs to do, ever
- *partial rejects:* the tasks that need to be done, but where you can be a whole lot smarter about how and when you do them.

What other women say

I make simple meals with great ingredients. I try to keep my closet simple and easy to maintain. I don't spend a lot of money or time on a beauty routine. And one that I'm a little ashamed of: I really only worry about birthdays of members of my immediate family. I've also rejected reality TV!

Amy Henry

I have spent a fortune over the years buying costumes for book week or Easter parades because I didn't have time to make them at home.

Kelly Grigsby

After my husband Zan died, I worked hard to rid myself of anything that made me stressed or anxious. These are such destructive emotions. I no longer think thoughts like, 'Did that come out wrong? Have I offended her?' I no longer worry what people think of me. I can't control that; all I can control are my actions.

Julie McDonald

When I took over as CEO, one of the first things I rejected was the established two-hour monthly executive team meetings that weren't achieving good outcomes. It just wasn't the best use of our team's time.

Rebecca Casson

A no-phones rule at the breakfast and dinner table and putting phones into airplane mode at 9 pm helps ensure we enjoy time with each other rather than zombieing out on our devices.

Sarah Wood

I use little to no social media. It has adverse effects on my professional life but I'm more focused and less anxious, which is worth the sacrifice.

Claire Hooper

In 2017 I went to Nepal and it was my first experience with living fully and simply. We now live very minimally, which makes for easy decision making.

Ali Villani

It's taken me a long time to figure it out: you don't have as much time as you think.

Joy Foster

EXERCISE 1: IT'S TIME TO REJECT THE TOTAL REJECTS

There is simply no valid reason you can give for continuing to invest time in the tasks you have identified on your time sheets as total rejects. These need to go—now.

Examples of total rejects on the home front include:

- piling instead of filing
- going to the supermarket at lunchtime every single day
- running errands in peak hour
- ironing bed linen (or for me, ironing full stop)

- checking your junk mail—it's called junk for a reason
- checking your phone every few minutes.

One of my favourite total rejects of all time was shared by a very classy female entrepreneur from the audience when I was the keynote speaker at an event in London. After sharing a few examples of total rejects, I asked for shares from the audience of any habits on the home front that they now considered to be total rejects. Her hand went right up: 'I think I have a total reject?' she said with a questioning tone. 'I iron my bras and underwear.' Ummm, yes, that is a total reject right there.

You have your list of total rejects. Take a deep breath because these stop right now—every time you catch yourself indulging in a total reject, ever again, stop.

What other women say

I need to do something about the number of meetings I go to. I have been known to arrange two lunches a day just to fit all of my meetings in! And that pretty much sums up my life.

Carmel Mulhern

I definitely have problems in this area, but I've started using a very simple technique: I imagine the rush of relief I will feel after saying no and lo and behold it's suddenly very easy to say.

Claire Hooper

EXERCISE 2: IT'S TIME TO REJECT THE PARTIAL REJECTS

Partial rejects are the tasks that need to be done, but you just need to be smarter about how and when you do them. Here's how.

- *Automate:* Identify the partial rejects you can build a process around or automate. For an initial, short-term time investment to automate the task, you will save a lot of time in the future. This is time well spent. Examples of tasks you can automate at home include:

  - setting up an online supermarket shopping list/weekly order online for delivery
  - online banking/auto payments/renewals/direct debits.

- *Batch:* Identify the partial rejects that have to be done, but which can be done in bulk as opposed to randomly here and there. Batch a weekly appointment with yourself in your calendar to deal with these tasks in bulk. Examples of tasks that should be batched include:

  - paying bills
  - sending invoices
  - reading and signing school notes
  - making a weekly meal plan and shopping list
  - cooking in bulk and freezing half for another night.

Wants

Finally, you've made it! This is where you get to do all the awesome things you *want* to do with your extra 30 plus hours a month. Your Wants are otherwise known as Me First, just in case that's a concept you have never given consideration to.

The great thing about working through The 5 SMART Steps is that other possibilities might have opened up to you: new ideas about what you can do with your reclaimed time, now that you have extra time.

EXERCISE 1: WANTS — I WANT IT, I WANT IT, I WANT IT!

Update your Wants list and keep it with you so you can add to it every time a new idea strikes you.

Lock your Wants into your calendar, make sure you turn up and give yourself permission to enjoy yourself without guilt.

What other women say

I have a balance sheet. On one side I have the things that really matter to me, such as handstand club, cardio, yoga and IV drips. The kids aren't scheduled in as they are at the core of what I do. I look at the balance sheet every day to see if I'm winning or losing and I adjust accordingly. Everything is scheduled.

Geeta Sidhu-Robb

I was on the US archery team for four years from 2004 to 2007, and I rowed before that at university and high school. And now I'm training for a marathon and Ironman. I have learned that my business does better when I'm in training.

Joy Foster

Let's check in on Alice.

Alice

Okay, this is where I'm at:

- Insourcing list is done. Held a family meeting and the kids, somewhat reluctantly, agreed that it was probably a good idea that they chip in to help around the house. Not least because Mom is at her wit's end and might just spontaneously combust if help is not forthcoming. The white board is magnificent and takes pride of place on the kitchen bench right next to the fridge so no-one can miss it.
- I also made three copies of the insourcing list, laminated them to make them indestructible, and placed them strategically around the house (blue-tacked to Henry's bedroom wall; blue-tacked to Olive's bedroom wall; and in the bathroom — where most

of the stuff seems to live in small, self-sustaining communities). Considered tacking one to John's head, but refrained when he openly declared what a good idea my insourcing list was. Bless him.

- I have shown John how to hang up his towel properly — poor man, seemed somewhat bewildered. More so, I have reminded him where the laundry is and demonstrated how the dirty clothes drawer next to the washing machine is very easy to pull out and deposit his dirty clothes in. Given it is only five or six steps from the bedroom floor to the laundry, I am confident he can make the journey each day without getting lost. So far, so good.
- I am still struggling to turn a blind eye to all the crap that lies around. I do catch myself picking it up and removing it. However, there have been an increasing number of occasions where I have just kicked the wet towels from my path, summoned all of my willpower and walked on.
- The general family chores have been divided between the kids. Just this week I have added the nights John will cook (and the kids will clean up) and the nights I will cook (and the kids will clean up).
- After much negotiation, I capitulated and agreed to pay the kids pocket money each week to do the general chores. I think this will help keep them motivated, plus they needed a bit of a win on this, the poor down-trodden little children.
- I have had to remind the kids every single day to do their chores. Feel like a whinging old mole — am I yelling more than I was before I started this process? How much longer before it is no longer a chore for me to get the kids to do their chores? Need to hang in there. The one chore that is regularly working without a reminder is feeding the pets, so it is starting to work.
- Hired a housekeeper. Yes I did! Life changing. Really. John and I did have one massive fight over the housekeeper because he only wanted her to come once

(continued)

Alice (*cont'd*)

a fortnight and I wanted her to come once a week. In the end we agreed to make it fortnightly on a trial basis.

- Rejects done — they were actually easy to implement, so I virtually wiped them all out at once. What will be more challenging is making sure they don't creep back into my day — this is a WIP.
- I have started meditation class. Ommm. Oh, and I have read a book.

Reflection

Great work! Now you know:

- exactly what your Musts are
- how and what you are going to Delegate—outsource
- how and what you are going to Delegate—insource
- how and what you are going to Reject
- what you are going to do with the time you are about to get back.

It's time to *take control.*

Step 5
Take control

Time is the one asset we all have exactly the same amount of and no-one, no matter how wealthy, stealthy or sneaky, can buy or steal more of it. And this is precisely why we need to move away from a mindset that time needs to be *managed*. Your time is money, and just like your money, it needs to be consciously and wisely *invested* for the greatest possible return. For the greatest possible bang for your buck.

You already know this — time is there to be invested, not managed (and definitely not wasted).

Today, the first thing you are going to invest your time in is reflecting on how far you have already come. You have worked through the first four of The 5 SMART Steps and you have:

- identified your key time challenges
- identified your core values
- mapped a few days of your life in detail
- considered what a better day would look like
- gained a true understanding of the four cost lenses
- identified which of the four costs resonates most strongly with you

- determined your Musts, Wants, Delegates and Rejects
- rejected your total rejects
- set up smarter systems for your partial rejects
- started outsourcing
- started insourcing
- started to put yourself first by locking in some Me Time.

Congratulations—you have officially taken control of your time! You have already proven that you *can* instil new habits. Now you need to sustain the changes you have made.

Maintaining momentum

Gyms stay in business for one reason, and one reason only: they have a lot of unmotivated members who initially joined up with very good intentions of regularly exercising, but who over time lost momentum and now rarely use their memberships. It is a business model built on having as many clients fail as possible. Look at it this way: if everyone who joined your local gym turned up day in and day out ready to exercise, your local gym would go out of business. It would not have enough space, treadmills, bikes and weights to meet the demands of all of its eager beaver, well-buffed clients.

As a successful professional woman, you have not built your success banking on working with unmotivated clients. You have built your success by setting goals, driving hard to win and staying motivated.

The same goes for transforming your time.

But, like a gym membership that rarely gets used, you might experience moments of procrastination and frustration when implementing The 5 SMART Steps and you might even want to give up. It's how you respond to these moments that will mark you out. No-one said it would be easy.

It's all about your mindset. It's all about Repetition, Consistency and Recalibration:

- *Repetition:* The more you repeat your new time habits (and the more you stop repeating your crazy old time habits) the more ingrained your new time behaviours will become. We all know this stuff. Perfect practice makes perfect. Keep your eye on the prize. And again, repetition means repeating your own new behaviours, and regularly reminding your family to repeat their new behaviours.

- *Consistency:* It's important to be consistent. Not just for your own wee tired brain, but for those around you who you are trying to re-program. For example, if you explain to your son that from now on he must clean his room before you will drive him to football training, you need to be consistent. If you enforce the rule twice and then the next time you let the rule slide because he is running late for training, you are sending your son mixed messages. And, like any kid with an ounce of spunk, when you next try to enforce the rule your son will (rightly) respond along the lines of, 'But Muuuuuum, you let me go to training last time without cleaning up! Can't I just do it later*?' [*Your son's definition of 'later' = 'never'. Because now he knows that he has you on the ropes, he will leave his room a mess for so long that eventually you will give up and do it yourself *or* his floordrobe may well grow legs and walk itself to the laundry.]

- *Recalibration:* You will become so good at managing your Musts, Delegates and Rejects that you will get back additional time to do more of what you love—the Wants. Continue to revisit your Musts, Wants, Delegates and Rejects because as you gain momentum you will realise there are more changes to make and more hours to reclaim. You will also need to recalibrate as your priorities or life circumstances change. This has certainly been the case for me.

What other women say

I maintain momentum by setting deadlines — read it, do it, enjoy it — and I ask myself, 'How am I going to feel if I don't do it? How will I feel if I do do it?'

Julie McDonald

I boast to people, mostly my husband, about my progress. And then I have to save face by following through on my big talk.

Claire Hooper

I write lists every weekday and stick to them. I imagine how fabulous the end result will feel even if it's painful to get there. I also use a trick that works during fun runs: when you're in the middle of it and things feel hard, imagine how you'll feel when you see family and friends at the finish line.

Kate Halfpenny

The 5 SMART Steps is an iterative process. I developed the framework after leaving full-time work as an executive to be a full-time mom. I then reframed again when I started my own business and needed to manage the juggle of establishing a business with being a mom. Three years ago, after my marriage ended and I found myself as a single mom with three teenagers and a business, I reframed again.

I met my husband when I was 23 and we married when I was 24. No marriage separation is easy. Everyone told me that the first year would be the toughest. For me, the first two years were horrendous. People play certain roles in a marriage: there is a division of labour that just seems to happen, based on skills, strengths and interests. One of the tasks that I had no interest in at all was our finances. I just floated along and let my husband take care of all that. As a consequence, when we separated I had very little idea of what money went where, how much we owed, to whom it was owed and where all the money was. I did not even know how to open a bank account—I rang a friend who is in banking and I cried to her down the phone at the depth of my financial ignorance. I was furious at myself for having been so financially complacent for the vast majority of my life.

Properly understanding my money shifted overnight from something I had always delegated (insourced) to my husband, to an absolute must for me. And so I reframed.

It was a steep learning curve. I changed banks. I found an accountant who was patient and taught me my numbers. I engaged a bookkeeper. I asked a lot of questions. I then opened bank accounts for each of my kids and started to teach them about their finances and managing their money.

In addition, my core values had a sudden and jarring shift. From now on it was primarily all about my kids and making sure I was completely available at a time of enormous upheaval for them. It was also about my business. I had lost the safety net of having a partner in full-time employment earning good money—from now on, the buck stopped with me, literally.

And although I had been plunged into a nightmare, The 5 SMART Steps was a lifebuoy for me. The framework helped remove some of the emotion from reframing and redesigning what my new life needed to look like because it was a practical, logical, step-by-step approach I could take to making new decisions for my new life with a level of confidence. It allowed me to focus exclusively on my kids and on my business and it ensured that I said *no* to everything else. This worked very well for the first three years after my husband left.

More recently, my mom passed away and this has caused me to again review my core values and where I choose to invest my time. Yes, I am a great mom and yes, I have a great business, but by channelling 100 per cent of my time and energy into these two endeavours over the past three years, I lost sight of also taking care of myself. And so I returned to The 5 SMART Steps to reframe again. The changes I have made with this iteration have been quite drastic and certainly impactful, and just right for what I need for me right now, including:

- having calculated exactly how many days I need to work each month in order to make the money I need to live the lifestyle I want for me and my kids
- having locked these days into my calendar and the rest is time for me to spend with my dad, my children and on myself
- focusing on my passions, such as good sleep, exercise and reading. I have enrolled in a course to learn Italian and I have a three-year plan to move and work overseas. Every time I have a speaking engagement in a new location I am tacking on two days just for me. I outsourced cleaning a long time ago, but I have now outsourced the pool maintenance and the garden. I am starting to put myself first.

My point in sharing this is that SMART time investment is an iterative process. You will need to revisit how and where you spend your time on a regular basis because life will throw you curve balls and you need to be able to adjust on the run. The 5 SMART Steps will help you do that.

PART III
How about a little bonus?

Now that you have hours of time back in your time budget, let's set some truly audacious personal and professional goals for where you are going to invest this time. This is important: you do not want to waste your reclaimed time by just frittering it away and nor do you want to waste your reclaimed time shooting for vanilla goals (no-one ever changed their life, or the world, shooting for vanilla).

How to set and smash audacious goals

It's time to move from the passenger seat to the driver's seat in your life—after all, this is what *Me First* is all about. Goal setting is an unbelievably powerful way to do this, and it will also help you:

- gain clarity over the long-term vision for your life
- gain a powerful injection of short-term motivation
- prioritise tasks
- stay single-focused, determined and single-minded
- reject what is wasting your time
- delegate what someone else can do faster, better and cheaper than you
- say 'no' to distractions.

It is really worth taking the time to do this right because the research is clear: the act of considering, writing down and then sharing your goals means you are more likely to achieve your goals.

> **What other women say**
>
> I have New Year's Resolutions, but inevitably they fall away. I think I need to have real goals rather than aspirational goals.
>
> **Carmel Mulhern**

Goal setting with The 5 SMART Steps

Let's set your audacious five-year goals. The 5 SMART Steps framework that you are now familiar with can also be used to help you set and smash your goals.

EXERCISE 1: SELF-AWARE

Your goals need to closely align to your values. You already know that having absolute clarity over the values that drive you is central to deciding where you should—and should not—invest your time. This is great news because you have already done a lot of work on your values and you know exactly what they are!

1 List your values here:

----

2 With your values in mind, write a statement below describing where you want to be in five years' time for each big-picture life goal:

My career/business:

My finances:

My family:

My lifestyle:

My personal development:

My health:

Other:

----

3 Against each statement write one to three reasons *why* this future state is important to you.

EXERCISE 2: MAP

At first glance, your five-year goals can seem overwhelming. How on earth are you supposed to achieve something so utterly audacious? Where on earth do you even start?

The answer is to break your big, audacious goals down into smaller, actionable steps—your short-term goals—which when combined will add up to achieving your big, audacious goals.

For example, your five-year health goal may be to run the New York Marathon. In order to achieve this goal in five years' time, you can't just rock up to the starting line in New York in your gym gear and hope for the best. There are so many moving parts to this goal, including building a training schedule, creating a nutrition plan, submitting an application for a spot in the race, coordinating time out from work, travel arrangements, accommodation arrangements, building a holiday around the race, flying your personal cheer squad with you, coordinating your cheer squad's time off school/work and so on.

This is where mind mapping comes in.

Physically map out (on a white board or butchers paper or using a mind-mapping app) your big-picture life goals and then break each goal down into smaller, bite-sized tasks. Capture every single step you know you have to take in order to achieve each goal. The more you break this down the better, because you are turning an overwhelmingly big goal into multiple, very doable, actionable tasks.

EXERCISE 3: ANALYSE

Consider each of the small tasks—your short-term goals—identified in your mind map and transcribe the mind-mapped outcomes onto your to-do list, written as an action:

- Allocate a deadline to each task.

- Remember Parkinson's Law—allocating a deadline to each task will significantly increase the likelihood of you completing the task and each time you do so, you will be creating an ongoing sense of momentum towards achieving your big-picture goals.
- Where there is alignment between tasks, batch them together in your calendar to be actioned in one batch of time and lock the batch into your calendar.

EXERCISE 4: REFRAME

You have articulated your five-year goals at a high level, mapped out each task you need to perform in order to achieve your goals and locked deadlines into your calendar. Now it's time to reframe/finesse your goals to ensure you are positioning yourself for maximum success.

When you reframe your goals you want each goal to be written in a way that is:

- *positive*—it's a funny thing the way we think. Sometimes, we think about the future and express our goals in a way that reflects a negative state of mind 'right now'. This is not helpful because you are essentially framing your future in a way that clearly illustrates that you are judging your present. For example, when it comes to health you may have written a goal such as, 'I want to run a marathon and lose 10 kilos.' What this goal says about you is that you currently think you are overweight, and that's not a helpful, positive frame of mind to be in when chasing down your goals.
- *expressed in the present tense*—you want to express your five-year goals in the present tense, as if they have already been realised. Doing so engenders a positive and motivated mindset and a strong sense of confidence about your future, and it helps you visualise exactly how your future looks and feels.

- *measurable*—you need to know when you have achieved your goal. Having a goal without measures or milestones means you will never know when you have succeeded. As you hit each milestone, celebrate! Once a milestone is achieved, either set a new goal or reframe your milestones/measures so that you continue to stretch yourself.

Take each of your goals from exercise 1 and rewrite the goal in a way that is (i) positive, (ii) written in the present tense and (iii) measurable.

For example, if your health goal was, 'I want to run a marathon and lose 10 kilos', you could rewrite your health goal as, 'In [insert date five years from now] I have just run the New York Marathon and my partner and kids were there to cheer me across the line! It is the best day of my life! By July [next year] I walk 10 000 steps a day, every single day—rain, hail or shine. This means I am burning over 1000 calories a day. By September [next year] I am running five kilometres a day. My blood pressure has measurably dropped and I am looking and feeling terrific!'

My career/business:

My finances:

My family:

My lifestyle:

My personal development:

My health:

Other:

EXERCISE 5: TAKE CONTROL

Having reframed your five-year goals, write them up and place them somewhere you can read them and spend a few minutes visualising them every single day. Focus on how you will feel when the goal is realised. This is the long game.

Each day you can refer to the bite-sized tasks from your master to-do list, which you have locked into your calendar as a deadline (your short-term goals) to ensure you are always working towards your big-picture goals.

Note (this is really important): Don't lose sight of the fact that we rarely follow a straight line towards achieving our goals—in fact, the tangents, turns and opportunities that arise simply by virtue of the goals we set out to achieve can often be more important, impactful and satisfying than the goals we originally set.

Always be alert to these opportunities as they arise so you are ready to act on and seize them.

Track your progress and celebrate the journey—not just the destination.

What other women say

I have 12-month goals, a five-year plan and a 10-year plan. I reflect on them regularly and it's important to have the courage to adjust. Recently I realised my 12-month 'financial' goal should be expressed as a 'people' goal. Ultimately, the outcome will probably be the same, but focusing on my team feels so much more authentic.

Angie Weston

Each morning after meditating, I set three goals for the day – a mixture of what I will do and how I am going to be. I also exercise regularly, which keeps me calm. My current goal is to be even more present and mindful in each interaction.

Tracey Slatter

Each day I ask, 'What is the ***one*** thing I want to achieve today?' and I make sure I have the time and headspace to make it a reality (it could be speaking at an event, having a difficult conversation with a colleague, attending the school concert, calling my mom) even if that means cancelling other stuff. At the end of each day, if I've achieved that ***one*** goal then I feel at peace with myself.

Sarah Wood

The simple act of writing a goal down seems to set me on the right path.

Caroline Jean-Baptiste

I remind myself of my end goal. I can be very consistent when my end goal is really important to me – even in the face of adversity.

Lucy Kippist

I break projects down into smaller tasks/steps to maintain momentum. It also helps me to overcome feeling overwhelmed. I get a lot of satisfaction looking back and seeing the progress I have made. I do this with my team and find it's the only way to get things done.

Snezana Jankulovski

I continue to visualise the end goal. I break it down into milestones and when I reach each milestone I celebrate. The journey needs to be enjoyed.

Nicole Pennefather

When you have goals, and someone asks for your time, if that 'ask' doesn't align with or support your goals, then saying 'no' is easier.

Jane Hall

Where to now?

A final word from Alice, 90 days on.

Alice

Without question, I have more time. I have more than 30 hours back a month to do what I love. I am doing more work, spending quality time with my family and — importantly — making time just for me. Olive and Henry can see the difference — I overheard them talking about me and Olive actually said, 'Mom is fun!' I've always wanted to be fun.

I definitely feel a lot less guilt when I head off to work, knowing that tonight when I get home (to a clean house courtesy of our housekeeper, and a meal cooked by John) I can sit with the kids and help with their homework rather than rush out to the supermarket, run the vacuum over the floor, clean the toilets and make dinner.

And I feel no guilt at all when I sit down to family time. I still have some guilt about putting myself first, but funnily enough, the more I do it the easier it gets!

On the downside, I still have to keep on top of the kids and their chores. I can't tell you how tempting it is just to clean up their stuff myself. But, I am staying strong! Yelling a bit, but they are starting to get the message. John, on the other hand, is transformed in his ability to put his dirty clothes in the wash — my threats to not wash anything that wasn't put in the laundry did the trick.

We have a housekeeper, a mother's helper, a guy who mows the lawn — and it has changed my life and our family life.

(continued)

Alice (*cont'd*)

My biggest challenge is staying on top of the Rejects list. I thought this would be the easy bit! It's very tempting to fall into the habit of hitting the supermarket every day, so I had to compromise and go twice a week. We do one big shop a week, and then either John, the nanny or I do a second run for extra milk, bread and other stuff we need. It's not a total reject outcome, but it's better than what it was and it is working for us. Next step will be to set up online shopping.

I sometimes feel a little guilty about not going to Olive's dance class, but not that guilty. But get this: having seen me plan out my time the SMART way, Olive wanted to map her own values. And she identified 'dance' as something she was losing interest in, with a possible preference for — wait for it — soccer! I swear to God I had nothing to do with pointing out to her that we are more of a 'sporty family' than a 'dancing family'. Truly.

We have had two trips down the coast to 'surf' (if that's what you can call it). The kids were unbelievable, both pretty much standing up and catching a wave straight away. Little buggers. Must be something about having a lower centre of gravity. I was bloody hopeless, which John and the kids ***loved***: 'Look at how hopeless Mom is!' But when I finally stood up for about 30 seconds, they were delirious with joy. I haven't laughed so much for ages — so much so I wet myself, which happily kept the wetsuit nice and warm.

Date night continues. I am simply hair free in all the right places. Plus I have locked in a girls' weekend away — unbelievable.

I have set my five-year goals and they are truly audacious. In five years' time I will be 43 and I have such a positive frame of mind for how I am going to smash out my goals! Bring it on!

But, it's now time just for me — Me First — according to my to-do list, so I'm off for a run. I am Alice and I have transformed my time.

Enjoy putting yourself first—without guilt.

Kate x

About Kate

Kate Christie, Founder and CEO of Time Stylers, is a time investment specialist, global speaker and bestselling author. She is in the business of helping you find time. Lots of time.

Kate works with high-performing teams and individuals on maximising individual time spend and managing organisational drag through SMART time investment strategies. She has appeared on television, radio and in print as a leading commentator on time management and maximising work/life integration to ensure success across work, family, community and life.

With a reputation for helping her clients find 30 hours of lost time a month, Kate's focus is to ensure you are left educated, entertained and with a lasting impact on the way you choose to lead, live, work and play.

Me First is Kate's fourth book. With lots of information out there on time management, Kate wanted to write something unique, practical, and easy to read and implement.

Please connect with Kate at:
Mail: info@timestylers.com
Web: mefirstbook.com
Web: www.timestylers.com
LinkedIn: www.linkedin.com/in/kate-christie/
Facebook: www.facebook.com/kate.christie.92

Work with Kate

Time Stylers was founded in 2014 by Kate Christie to help you gain control of your time across your work, family, community and life. The Time Stylers approach is to combine coaching, education and productivity strategies to create, build and sustain a much smarter personal and business time investment framework to ensure you free up hours of your precious time.

Everything we do is intelligently, strategically and enthusiastically focused on maximising your time so you can live the life you love.

If you want to know more about how Kate can work with you individually or with your team to help you achieve awesome results, go to www.timestylers.com or send an email to info@timestylers.com with your contact details and we can discuss coaching, workshop and education options with you. Kate's products include:

- *speaker, emcee, workshop facilitator*—as a global keynote presenter, workshop facilitator and emcee, Kate's authenticity is one of her greatest assets; her focus is on ensuring your audience is left with a lasting impact on the way they choose to lead, live, work and play as a result of what they have learned. Kate's style is direct, practical, engaging, motivational and humorous. Your audience will walk away with a clear action plan on what they can do differently for immediate time gains. Kate has spoken to audiences including L'Oréal, Telstra, Westpac, Deloitte, PwC, QuickBooks, De Lorenzo, Cox Automotive, Australian Veterinary Association, National Dental Care, Mass Participation Asia and the European Enterprise Network, to name a few.

- *board, C-suite and senior management briefings*—Kate provides briefings to board directors, C-suite and senior managers about productivity, the associated cost savings of getting productivity right, and time management as a key workplace occupational health and safety risk. She offers one-off briefings as well as retainer/ongoing advisory services to help ensure companies maximise productivity outcomes and minimise costs and other risks.
- *business/team workshops*—SMART time investment workshops are tailored to the specific needs of your business/team and each individual in the team, and include:
  - a pre-workshop survey to identify key time investment challenges
  - a guided pre-workshop individual time audit
  - all materials
  - a written report on survey data.
- *executive/business coaching*—Kate specialises in helping successful, time-poor professionals, business owners, educators and entrepreneurs manage their time smarter. Her 1:1 executive/business coaching is targeted at high-performing individuals to help them take their success to the next level.
- *SMART time investment licensing*—Kate provides your organisation with a SMART time investment licence to use her framework, The 5 SMART Steps, including up-skilling your own internal team to train others across your organisation on The 5 SMART Steps framework.

- *a DIY 30 day time transformation program*—an online, self-paced, do-it-yourself program specifically designed to help business owners and entrepreneurs invest their time with intent for greater success. Content includes:
  - Kate Christie's ebook, *The SMART Time Investment Workbook*
  - daily emails from Kate for 30 days with instructions, advice, tips, implementation guidance and motivation
  - daily vlogs from Kate for 30 days
  - an action plan
  - tools and templates
  - a time tracker.
- *books and free resources*—Kate is the best-selling author of four time investment books. She also has a range of fantastic free time investment templates, tools and resources (for both your business and home) that you can access at www.mefirstbook.com and www.timestylers.com/resources/.

Acknowledgements

Thank you to everyone who provided support and guidance while I was writing *Me First* and special thanks to every woman who generously gave her time to contribute her thoughts and personal experience to *Me First*—whether quoted or not.

Index

Acharya, Anu 31, 128, 142
Alice case study
—Analyse step 103, 106, 107–108, 111, 112–113, 114, 115, 116–117, 118
—cost lenses 111, 112–113, 114, 115, 116–117, 118
—goals 172
—insourcing 137–138, 141, 148–150
—Map step 90–91, 93–96. 98–100
—outsourcing 129–130, 171
—Reframe step 129–130, 137–138, 141, 148–150, 172
—rejecting 148–150
—Self-aware step 61–62, 68–69, 70, 74, 81–82, 86–87
—SMART steps 51–53, 60, 171–172
—values 81–82, 83–84, 86–87
Allis, Janine 22, 31, 34, 73, 76, 85
Analyse step 58, 103–120; *see also* cost lenses, four; delegate; musts; reject; wants
—Alice 103, 106, 107–108, 111, 112–113, 114, 115, 116–117, 118
—categories of tasks 103, 104–108
—categorise exercise 105–106
—cost lenses 109–119
—costs exercise 110–115
—delegate 58, 62, 104–105, 106, 107, 121
—emotions exercise 117–118
—goal setting exercise 164–165
—insourcing 105
—musts 58, 104
—musts vs wants 116–117

Analyse step (*continued*)
—outsourcing 104
—real cost of habits 108
—reclaimed time 107–108
—reject 58, 105, 106, 107, 121
—savings, calculating total 118–119
—stress testing categories exercise 116–117
—timesheets 105
—wants 58, 104
anxiety 7, 26

boiling frog 15
burnout 42
busy lifestyle syndrome (BLS) 9–13, 44, 62, 68
—solution 16
—women's comments 15, 16

Carter, Christine Michel 13
case study *see* Alice case study
Casson, Rebecca 7, 30, 33, 63, 76, 144
children *see also* delegating; motherhood
—household chores 36, 37–38, 134, 135, 136, 139, 140, 143, 148–149
—as manipulators 37–38, 155
collaboration 59
comparisons 9, 18–19, 20
competition 18, 78
connecting 12, 35, 65, 123, 130
cost lenses, four 109–119
—Alice 111, 112–113, 114, 115, 116–117, 118
—defined 109
—emotional 109, 114
—financial 109, 110–112
—opportunity 109, 112–113
—physical 109, 115
—stress testing categories exercise 116–117
—women's comments 112, 113

data, value of 16, 57–58, 89
delegating 25, 157 *see also* children; insourcing; outsourcing
—Analyse step 58, 62, 104–105, 106, 107, 121
—family and 121–122
—insourcing 39, 105, 130–142, 148–149, 157
—outsourcing 104, 124–130, 171
—in reframing 121, 122, 123–144
demands, competing 57–58
doing it all 36, 37–38, 52, 127, 136, 141, 142, 155
doing it yourself 36, 136, 155; *see also* delegating; insourcing; outsourcing
Depledge, Alexandra 11, 18, 30, 35, 41, 114, 127

faking it *see* imposter syndrome
family meeting exercise 139–141
feedback, dealing with negative 26, 30–31
financial budget 23
5 SMART Steps *see* SMART Steps, five; *see also* entries under names of individual steps 1–5
Foster, Joy 22, 46, 144, 148

gender balance 52
gender divide 43
goals 159–172
—Alice 172
—analyse exercise 164–165
—audacious 159, 161–162
—map exercise 164
—reframe exercise 165–167
—self-aware exercise 162–163
—setting own 19, 161–162
—setting with 5 SMART steps 162–169
—take control exercise 167–168
—women's comments 168–169
—writing 165–169
good enough, not *see* imposter syndrome
Grigsby, Kelly 7, 10, 28, 33, 43, 86, 121, 128, 144
guilt 7, 27, 32–35, 60, 68, 77, 82, 87, 114; *see also* judgement
—solution 33–34
—women's comments 33, 34–35

Halfpenny, Kate 19, 25, 27, 34, 65, 113, 156
Hall, Jane 16, 25, 169
Hatzitefanis, Maria 18, 35, 78
having it all 3, 17, 40–41
—solution 40–41
—women's comments 41
help, not needing 42–43; *see also* children; delegating; insourcing; outsourcing; partner
—solution 42–43
—women's comments 43
Henry, Amy 11, 19, 28, 33, 128, 142, 144
Hooper, Claire 64, 144, 146, 156
household chores 36, 37–38, 52, 127, 134, 135–137, 141, 142, 148–149, 155; *see also* children; delegating; insourcing; outsourcing

imposter syndrome 7, 9–13, 17
—solution 12–13
—women's comments 10–11, 13

insourcing 39, 105, 130–142, 143, 148–149, 157; *see also* children; delegating; partner
—Alice 137–138, 141, 148–150
—children 130, 131–134, 135–137, 138–139
—communication 131
—family as a team sport 130, 131, 133–134, 139–142
—family meeting exercise 139–141
—individual 131–133
—method of 130
—partner 135, 136, 139, 140, 143
—SMART method of 142–144
—traps in 135–139
—two types 131–134
—women's comments 135, 142

Jankulovski, Snezana 18, 22, 30, 64, 76, 129, 135, 169
Jean-Baptiste, Caroline 14, 15, 28, 73, 113, 142, 168
Jenkins, Kate 16, 20, 41, 64, 72, 86, 113
judgement 3–4, 7, 26–31, 96; *see also* guilt
—dealing with 29–30
—solution, feedback 30–31
—solution, judgement 28–30
—vs feedback 30
—women's comments 27–28, 31

kids *see* children
Kippist, Lucy 16, 22, 30, 85, 169

McDonald, Julie 11, 15, 27, 33, 76, 114, 128, 135, 144, 156
McKeown, Meg 11
mapping time 57–58
Map step 16, 57–58, 89–101
—Alice 90–91, 93–96. 98–100
—competing demands 57
—data, importance of 57–58, 89
—dream day 97–100
—exercises 91–100
—goal-setting exercise 164
—time audit 89
—time sheet examples 93–96, 98–100
—time sheets 91–93, 97–98
—typical day 91–96
marriage and work 45–46; *see also* motherhood
maternity leave 6, 26, 32
meetings 57, 61, 62, 63, 97, 104, 123, 145, 146
mindset, reactive to active 51
mistakes we make 1–47
Moras, Nicola 72
motherhood *see also* delegating;

guilt; judgement; maternity leave
—career 5–7, 32, 33, 34, 45–46, 71, 77, 82–83, 85, 108, 114, 117
—changing rules 4, 5–6
—child care 6, 45, 82–83
—effects of 5, 7, 10, 26
—emotional costs 114–115
—guilt 26–27, 32, 117, 172
—household chores 36, 37–38, 52, 135–137, 141, 142, 155
—judgement 3–4, 26–27
—new rules 4, 5
—primary carer 6, 26, 43
—responses to 3–4
—winging it 9–10
—women's comments 7
Mulhern, Carmel 15, 20, 22, 25, 31, 47, 80, 114, 127, 135, 146
multitasking 53, 90
musts *see also* wants
—Analyse step 58, 104
—defined 122
—Reframe step 122–123
—vs wants 116–117

negative, dealing with 26

opportunities 12, 21
outsourcing 104, 124–130, 171; *see also* delegating; inspourcing
—Alice 129–130, 171
—batching tasks 129
—examples 124–126
—exercise 127–130
—template for 127
—women's comments 127–129

Parkinson's Law 44
partner 62, 73, 84; *see also* motherhood
—childcare 6
—insourcing 135, 136, 139, 140, 143, 149
—problem of 39
—solution to problem of 39
perfection 1, 9, 17, 27, 139
pregnancy 4–5
priorities 21, 24–25, 46, 58, 71, 72, 75, 114, 77, 78, 82–83, 84–85, 86, 114, 155, 161

Reframe step 59, 121–151 *see also* delegating; insourcing; outsourcing
—Alice 129–130, 137–138, 141, 148–150, 172
—delegate 121, 122, 123–144
—explained 121–122
—goal-setting exercise 165–167
—habits 122
—musts 122–123
—refining choices 123, 147, 155
—reject 121, 122

Reframe step (*continued*)
—revisiting the framework 59
—wants 122, 147–150
—wants exercise 147–150
—women's comments 121
rejecting 25, 121–122, 144–147
—Alice 148–150
—batching 147
—partial rejects 105, 144, 146–147
—total reject examples 145–146
—total rejects 105, 144, 145–146
—women's comments 144–145, 146, 148

Self-aware step, 68–69 56–57, 61–88; *see also* values, defining your
—Alice 61–62, 68–69, 70, 74, 81–82, 86–87
—changing one thing 70–72
—drivers, your 56–57, 75–86
—emotional state 65–67
—goal-setting exercise 162–163
—pain points 63–64, 70
—prioritising self 71
—values, defining your 57, 75–86
—want, what you really 71–72
—wants list 72, 73–75
—women's comments 64–65, 72, 73, 76, 78, 80, 85–86
self-care 34, 46, 58, 71–72, 114, 148, 157, 165; *see also* priorities
self-confidence 26
self-doubt 4, 7, 9, 10, 11, 12, 19
self-reflection 61, 62, 63, 70, 71, 86
selflessness, epidemic of 46
self-sufficiency 136, 142
Sidhu-Robb, Geeta 43, 47, 128, 148
Slatter, Tracey 11, 18, 65, 168
SMART Steps, five 36, 46, 49–158; *see also* entries under names of individual steps 1–5
—1 Self-aware 56–57, 61–88
—2 Map 16, 57–58, 89–101
—3 Analyse 58, 103–120
—4 Reframe 59, 121–151
—5 Take control 59, 153–158
—6th step 59
—Alice and the 51–53, 60, 61–62, 68–69, 70, 74, 81–82, 86–87, 90–91, 93–96. 98–100, 103, 106, 107–108, 111, 112–113, 114, 115, 116–117, 118, 129–130, 137–138, 141,

148–150, 171–172
—commitment to 56
—goal setting with 162–169
—overview 55–60
—purpose of 49
—reiterative process 153–158
social media 9, 91, 145
start, don't know where to 44
—solution 44
stress 60, 68
superwoman syndrome 7, 17–20
—solution 18–19
—women's comments 18, 19–20
support network 41

Take control step 59, 153–158
—consistency 155
—example, finance 156–157
—goal-setting exercise 167–168
—gym example 154
—momentum, maintaining 154–158
—recalibration 155
—reframing 147, 156–157
—repetition 155
—women's comments 156
time, investing *see also* financial budget
—consistency 155
—improving 1, 37
—mindset, shifting your 8
—mistakes made 1
—overspending 23
—recalibration 155
—repetition 155
—vs managing 55–56, 153
time for me 45–47
—solution 46
—women's comments 46–47
time sheets 91–93, 97–98
—examples 93–96, 98–100
time wasting 3–8
truth 24

values, identifying your 23, 57, 75–86, 114, 157–158
—Alice 81–82, 83–84, 86–87
—examples of 76–77, 80
—exercises for 78–86
—goals and 162
—most important 79–80
—prioritising 84–86
—reflection 83, 86
—top 82–84
—trade-offs 84–85
—women's comments 76, 78, 80, 85–86
Villani, Ali 46, 145

wants
—exercise 147–150
—list 72, 73–75
—Reframe step 122, 147–150
—Self-aware step 72, 73–75

wants (*continued*)
—vs musts 58, 104
—what you really want 71–72
Weston, Angie 7, 25, 27, 33, 41, 73, 86, 128, 168
Wood, Sarah 19, 31, 34, 78, 131, 142, 144, 168
work-life balance vs integration 40–41

yes syndrome 21–25
—saying no 24, 25
—solution 22–25
—traps in 21
—women's comments 22, 25